ARKANSAS NATURE LOVER'S GUIDEBOOK

HOW TO FIND 101 SCENIC AREAS IN "THE NATURAL STATE"

TIM ERNST

W0010692

www.TimErnst.com

TIM ERNST PUBLISHING
PETTIGREW, ARKANSAS

The cover photo of cypress trees was taken by the author at Apple Lake, Dagmar Wildlife Management Area, in The Big Woods region (page 158).

Library of Congress Control Number: 2006906821
ISBN: 9781882906581

Book designed by Tim Ernst, maps drawn by Pam Ernst
Other production team members include Amber Dedmon, Don Kurz,
Judy Ferguson, Ron Ferguson, and Angela Filbeck

Other publications by Tim Ernst
Arkansas Waterfalls guidebook
Arkansas Hiking Trails guidebook
Buffalo River Hiking Trails guidebook
Ozark Highlands Trail guidebook
Ouachita Trail guidebook
Arkansas Dayhikes For Kids guidebook
Buffalo River Beauty picture book
Arkansas Landscapes II picture book
Arkansas Portfolio III picture book
Arkansas Autumn picture book
Arkansas Wildlife picture book
Arkansas Landscapes picture book
Arkansas Waterfalls picture book
Buffalo River Dreams picture book
Arkansas Portfolio II picture book
Arkansas Wilderness picture book
Buffalo River Wilderness picture book
Arkansas Spring picture book
Arkansas Portfolio picture book
Wilderness Reflections picture book
The Search For Haley
Cloudland Journal ~ Book One

Color prints of all photos in this guidebook,
and our publications are available from:
TIM ERNST PUBLISHING
www.TimErnst.com

Table Of Contents

Introduction

WELCOME to my scenic guide for nature lovers in Arkansas, The Natural State! This book is filled with treasure maps, photos, and descriptions to some of the most beautiful locations in the country. Bluffs, waterfalls, swamps, vistas, mountains, prairies, scenic drives, hiking trails, canoe trails, giant trees, trumpeter swans, elk and flocks of geese and bald eagles (plus tigers and elephants)—they're all here, and all you have to do is follow the directions. Some of the most popular scenic destinations are included, as well as many that have been difficult to find and seldom visited.

Each listing has a map, descriptive info, and a color photo to illustrate the area; plus quick-reference symbols and other info above each listing to let you know what type of area it is and how difficult. The scenic areas are grouped into six geographical regions of the state, with a reference map and alphabetical listing of areas at the beginning of each region (there is a list of all areas by region on the back cover). The areas are placed geographically in the book within each section so that you can easily find nearby areas.

There are many hundreds, perhaps even thousands of great scenic locations in Arkansas, and I obviously have not included them all here, nor even attempted to list a complete set of any particular type of scenic area. For instance, there are many more protected prairies and wildlife refuges in Arkansas than are listed here, but you will be able to get a good taste of what they're all about by visiting the ones in the book. Some areas are quite scenic all year long, while others will peak during blooming seasons but may also be interesting during other times of the year.

The locations that you find in this guidebook are the ones that I frequent in my quest to document the great natural beauty of Arkansas. I've been going to some of them for many years, while others I just discovered while doing research for this book (and will be going back to for many years to come!). Many of my recommendations stem from a photography point of view, but they are just as appropriate for anyone wanting to see the very best our state has to offer. Take a few minutes to read through this introduction and then browse the photos and start making a list.

A few notes about different types of scenic areas listed in this book.

BLUFFS and ROCK CLIMBING AREAS. We have some incredible tall bluffs in Arkansas that are often streaked and painted with minerals, and offer terrific scenic vistas. Many of the really great scenic bluff areas are frequented by rock climbers and if you find out about a favorite rock-climbing area, it probably will be worth a visit for the beauty as well. Some of our climbing areas are really popular and can draw hundreds of climbers from around the area during weekends (like Sam's Throne). Others are hardly used at all and offer solitude and great beauty at the same time. Naturally, all of these bluff areas can be quite dangerous if you are hiking along the tops and so extreme caution is urged while you are there. If you bring along your kids, be sure to hang onto them at all times!

I have made note of some vista locations along the tops of blufflines, but there certainly are lots more. Some of your best scenic views will be from the bottom of the bluffs—not only will you see the surface of the bluff from below but there are often caves and waterfalls to explore, and boulders strewn about along the base of the bluffs.

Sometimes there are hiking trails on top of or along the base of bluffs, but more often there will be no official trail and you will simply have to bushwhack around and find your way. Some bluffs are marked on the maps with a bluff symbol but many are not.

CAVES. We have hundreds of wild caves and dozens of commercial caves in Arkansas that vary from tiny and dull to huge and spectacular. There are three wild caves and three commercial caves listed in this guidebook. I picked a couple of really nice but small commercial caves (Cosmic Cavern and Mystic Caverns), plus the granddaddy of them all, Blanchard Springs Caverns, which rivals any commercial cave in the country. The smaller caves are perfect for first-time cavers, but save Blanchard for last. The wild caves are on popular hiking trails (Devil's Den and Eden Falls) and are short and easy to explore (one has a 30-foot waterfall in the back!). The other wild cave, Cave Mountain Cave, is for the more serious spelunker. You can get lost easily and get into serious trouble—know cave safety rules and go with experienced cavers if you visit this cave! Many wild caves are gated and closed to the public to protect delicate cave features and endangered species that live within. If you are really interested in exploring wild caves, your best bet is to join a local cave group or "grotto."

NATURE CENTERS and VISITOR CENTERS. We have had an explosion of new, multi-million dollar visitor and nature centers in Arkansas since the passage of the 1/8th of one percent sales tax, and my goodness these new centers are just wonderful! We'll have four large nature centers operated by the Arkansas Game and Fish commission in Pine Bluff, Jonesboro, Ft. Smith, and Little Rock; the great White River National Wildlife Refuge Visitor Center in St. Charles; a new Audubon Nature Center in Little Rock; and quite a few new state park visitor centers, including ones at Bull Shoals-White River State Park, Hobbs State Park-Conservation Area, Cossatot River State Park Natural Area, Mt. Magazine State Park, and Lake Dardanelle State Park with more to come! These centers will not only help you plan your visit and answer your questions, they offer a wide variety of educational and environmental programs throughout the year and have large centers with extensive exhibits and audio-visual aids, plus plenty of hiking trails outside. Oops, I almost forgot—we have two wonderful Elk Education Centers right here in Newton County where you can learn all about the wild elk and other wildlife of the area—one is located in Ponca and one right on Scenic Hwy. 7 in Jasper.

A popular trend these days is to name a facility after someone (often overriding a previous name), which creates all sorts of problems when it is time to list the facilities in alphabetical order in books like this one (on the back cover and in the regional section headings). Should the Janet Huckabee Arkansas River Valley Nature Center be listed under J, H, A, R, or N? There does not seem to be any standard way of doing this —the Fred Berry Conservation Education Center (that used to be called Crooked Creek Ed. Center) is listed under F by the Game and Fish Commission. Go figure. So most of the time I have ignored the person's name on the main lists and listed it under the more common name of the facility, but have kept the person's name in the title on each individual page.

PRAIRIES. We only have a few small plots left of the tens of thousands of acres of wild prairies that once covered much of Arkansas. These exist in protected parcels scattered across the state, and many of them are owned and managed by the Arkansas Natural Heritage Commission to protect the rare plants and critters that live there. Some prairies are located right in the middle of town, like Baker Prairie in Harrison, while others are out in the middle of nowhere, like Grandview Prairie in southwest Arkansas. And while the main reason these prairies are protected is for the rare species present, they also happen to explode each spring with carpets of wildflowers. Yes siree my friend, if you want to photograph wildflowers head to your nearest prairie! At first glance many prairies may appear dull, but when you get out of your car and walk around you will see there are tons of life there. Of course, they are best viewed in the spring and summer months when things are blooming, but some also take on brilliant fall color in October and November.

Sometimes the prairie will be covered with a particular species of wildflower for a couple of weeks, then that species will die off. Later another species will explode onto the scene for a little while and then die back. This process will repeat several times during the blooming season as different species come and go, and you may need to return to your favorite prairie often to catch the blooms just right. Any time spent in a prairie is time well spent.

SCENIC DRIVES. Just about our entire state is a scenic drive, but I have picked out five that really show off the best of Arkansas and are scattered around the state. The big one is Talimena Scenic Drive in the Ouachitas that stretches far into Oklahoma and has more than two dozen scenic vista parking areas along the way. Don Kurz does a wonderful job of describing this route in his *Scenic Driving The Ozarks* book, and so I just hit the high points (sorry for that pun). The gravel road Winona Forest Drive goes through the heart of the Ouachita mountains with plenty of great views. We have two great drives in the Ozarks—one winds through the historic Boxley Valley along the Buffalo River where you can see herds of wild elk; and the other is a gravel-road drive along one of my favorite waterfall photography routes, Falling Water Creek. We also have a scenic drive along a swamp, or bayou, Robe Bayou. This gravel road parallels the Robe Bayou Canoe Trail and provides some great views of the bayou right from the road.

SWAMPS and BAYOUS. I have always loved the idea and look of swamps but it was not until I started doing research for this guidebook several years ago that I was able to actually get "in" and enjoy swamps. What I discovered is that they are not nearly as mysterious and spooky as one might think, and they can be breathtakingly beautiful. In fact, some of the swamps listed in this guidebook are now on my top-ten list of most scenic spots in all of Arkansas. They're wonderful in the early spring (March through April) as the new growth appears with that great brilliant green. And while most folks would not think about fall color in a swamp, baldcypress and tupelo trees can produce some incredible fall color and should be at the top of your list in October and November. Many of the swamps have high water during the winter months and are best viewed in the spring, although I found quite a few great float trips during the summertime as well. If you can stand the cold and conditions are not too flooded, winter is a great time to be in the swamps since you can see so much farther with no greenery to get in the way. By the way, some of the "lakes" shown on the maps are filled with cypress and tupelo trees (like Goose Pond, Apple Lake, and Frazier Lake). I have tried to show some greenery around these lakes on the maps to indicate the potential for great swamp viewing.

One of the problems with swamps is that most of them are, well, swamps, which means you cannot walk across them easily. The best way to visit many of the swamps is via a canoe. Since I don't like to haul a boat around all the time I use an inflatable canoe that is perfect for impromptu swamp visits, and stows easily into a large bag in the back of the car. Many of the swamps are along well-defined rivers that are lined with cypress and tupelo trees and you probably won't get lost. However, there are many swamps that are vast areas of nothing but trees and water as far as you can see and it is easy to get lost. I use a GPS and mark a waypoint at the put-in point to make it easier to return.

Bayous are kind of like river swamps and they can go on for a long distance. A couple of famous ones in Arkansas are Bayou DeView (where the Ivory-billed woodpecker was first rediscovered in 2004), and Bayou Bartholomew (the longest bayou in the world). Both of these bayous contain some of the most beautiful cypress and tupelo forests in the state, and what a thrill it is to drift downstream with ancient 1000-year old giants towering above you. Bayous are indicated on the maps as blue rivers with some green around them. Bayous and swamps—I love them!

TRAILS. There are hundreds of great hiking, biking, horseback, ATV, and boating trails all over Arkansas. A few of the very best and most scenic hiking trails are included in this guidebook, along with some great canoe trails in the swamps. While some of these trails are also great for other uses too (like mountain biking and horseback riding), all of the descriptions here are written from either a hiker or canoeist's view simply because those are the activities that I do the most and are comfortable writing about. Check with the individual parks for information about other types of trails. NOTE: "bushwhacking" is hiking cross-country without a trail and can be extremely difficult (easy to get lost too!).

And if you enjoy hiking, consider picking up copies of our other trail guidebooks where you will find hundreds of other trails all over the state. Many of the trails listed in this guidebook have short trail descriptions due to space limitations, but will have lengthy descriptions in the other guidebooks.

WATERFALLS. We have hundreds of terrific waterfalls in the Ozark and Ouachita mountain regions, and many of the best ones are included in this guidebook. These are "wet weather" waterfalls and are at their best during the winter and spring months when there is normally plenty of rainfall. Most of them flow very little and even dry up during the summer and fall months, although sometimes we do get great waterfalls in the fall. If you are a true waterfall hunter, be sure to pick up a copy of my *Arkansas Waterfalls Guidebook*—that will keep you busy for a long time!

WILDERNESS AREAS, NATURAL AREAS, SCENIC AREAS. There are a lot of different types of "scenic areas" in Arkansas and sometimes it can get confusing. A "Wilderness Area" is a federally-owned area that has been set aside by Congress where no vehicles or any type of management activities are allowed (we have 14 true wilderness areas in Arkansas)—hiking, bushwhacking, camping, hunting and fishing, and other non-destructive activities are welcome. This is the highest level of protection we have. "Natural Areas" are specific areas set aside and managed by the Arkansas Natural Heritage Commission for the protection of rare and endangered species of fauna and flora and their habitat. There are more than 50 such areas all over the state, and include some very small tracts of important prairie lands and other delicate ecosystems. These special areas are often cooperatively managed with the Arkansas Game and Fish Commission, The Nature Conservancy, and other organizations. While they are not protected for their scenic qualities, they just so happen to have some really terrific scenic parts to them! There are several other types of scenic areas that have been designated, but these carry no permanent protection and are apt to change names at any time (like "Special Interest Areas"). For this reason I have labeled most of these areas simply as "Scenic Areas" which pretty much describes them to a tee (like the Dismal Hollow Scenic Area). I must admit that in at least one case (Dry Creek Scenic Area) where a particular area did not have a name attached to it I have labeled it as a "Scenic Area" because I felt it deserved it.

WILDLIFE MANAGEMENT AREAS and REFUGES. We have quite a few wonderful areas all across the state that have been set aside and managed specifically for wildlife. Some of these are owned and managed by the Arkansas Game and Fish Commission and are called "wildlife management areas." Others are owned and managed by the U.S. Fish and Wildlife Service and are called "national wildlife refuges." Many of these areas allow hunting during the regular or special hunting seasons, while some others do not allow hunting of any sort. If you plan to visit any of them during the fall when most hunting seasons happen, it is a good idea to contact the specific agency to see what their regulations are (phone numbers and web pages are included on each area map). There are literally dozens of these wildlife areas scattered all across the state, and I have selected what I consider to be some of the best to include here—get a copy of the *Arkansas Watchable Wildlife Guide* (published by Game and Fish) for listings of many other areas.

One of the benefits of managing wildlife for hunters is the fact that these areas contain not only large numbers of these game species but also a lot of other non-game wildlife species too and are perfect places for wildlife viewing. In fact, many of the areas have set up special wildlife viewing trails and even observation blinds and welcome the general public to come see the wildlife. Several of the areas also have visitor centers and these should be your first stop—they can tell you what wildlife is around and often the best places to see them, plus they have some pretty neat exhibits too. Unfortunately some of the visitor centers are not open on weekends, so be sure to call ahead for information.

Several of the wildlife areas specifically manage waterfowl, and often the lands are flooded during the winter migration season. Obviously, when these areas are flooded you will need a boat to get into them, so watch the water levels, call ahead, and plan accordingly. The White River National Wildlife Refuge will close many areas from December through February with no access allowed, and many refuge roads will be closed when there is high water—be sure to give them a call for the latest info before you head there.

Oh yes, one other thing about these wildlife areas—it just so happens that many of them contain vast areas of swampland and are some of the most scenic locations in the entire state!

I have also included a pair of unique wildlife refuges in this book where you can see exotic animals. One has more than 100 big cats (lions and tigers, but also species native to Arkansas like cougars, black bears, and bobcats) that have been rescued and given permanent homes (Turpentine Creek near Eureka Springs). The other is one of only two preserves in this country that cares for abandoned elephants (Riddle Elephant Sanctuary near Greenbrier). Both areas allow visitors and will give you a chance to see these incredible animals up close.

WILDLIFE VIEWING TIPS. While it is possible to simply get in your car and drive around and view wildlife (in fact that is a great way to do it), here are a few tips to give you the best chance to see wildlife. First off, get up EARLY and stay late. Most wild critters are active at night and in the early morning hours. Once the sun comes up a lot of them go to bed or go hide. The elk in Boxley Valley are a perfect example. Quite often they are out grazing in the open fields right next to the highway (Boxley Valley Scenic Drive), but when the sun comes up, poof, they're gone—they go back into the thick woods and you will not see them. But if you are there before sunup you may get to see quite a show (they also come out just before dark). Wear dark clothing and muted colors so that you are not as visible to wildlife. Move slowly. Be quiet. And be patient. If you prefer to view wildlife from your car, drive slow, have your binoculars or camera ready, and if you do spot wildlife, it is best to keep the motor running and roll down the window rather than stop the motor and get out—critters know all about cars and the people inside them!

Sometimes you have to sit and wait for wildlife to come to you, or to come into view. You may have startled them when you arrived, but if they are feeding or like that particular spot for some reason they may come back—you just have to sit down, be quiet and wait them out. I have found that when photographing wading birds, I have to develop a relationship with a particular bird—let them know I am OK and not a threat. They spook easily, but if I stand my ground and hang around a while, they will come back, closer and closer and eventually will return to their normal routine—that is when you can get some great photos!

Carry a pair of good binoculars. Wildlife is indeed "wild" and generally afraid of humans so you will seldom get a close up view of them. So pack your binocs and enjoy viewing from a distance. Speaking of keeping your distance, it is never a good idea to come in physical contact with wildlife (you or the wildlife might get hurt). Please don't feed them, disturb them, or disrupt their daily routine in any way.

Pick your season to maximize your chances of viewing wildlife. Some species are only here during their migrations north or south (think ducks and geese in the winter-time, songbirds in the spring and fall). Other species are less wary of humans and tend to live and play more out in the open at certain times of the year (like deer and their fawns in the early summertime). You are more likely to see critters in areas where there are higher concentrations of wildlife than others, like in the wildlife refuges and in state parks. Here are three of the best sure-thing wildlife spectacles that you can count on in the state: Trumpeter swans at Magness Lake in the winter, bald eagles and flocks of snow geese at Holla Bend in the winter, and bugling bull elk in Boxley Valley in late September.

Field guides are great to have along and will not only identify what you see but will also give you some tips about where and when to look for specific species. And speaking of where and when to look, your very best resource is to stop by or call the office or visitor center where you plan to visit and ask them for guidance—they are there to help!

A few notes about the book.

DIFFICULTY RATINGS. Many of the locations in this guidebook are easy to reach and suitable for kids, older folks, and anyone who may not be in the greatest of shape (or can be viewed without even getting out of the car!). Other areas require more strenuous effort to reach and should not be attempted by those with health issues or who are not comfort-able in a woods environment. There are a few of the more remote scenic spots listed here that should only be visited by those with expert backcountry skills, that are capable of re-ally difficult scrambling through rugged terrain for hours on end. At the top of each listing there is a note about the difficulty and type of travel needed that you can use as your guide, as in: Easy/medium/difficult hiking or bushwhacking (remember bushwhacking is hiking cross-country without trails, and is generally more difficult than hiking on a maintained trail, although I love it!); canoe; caving; or auto. You also need to take the distance into consideration, so that is listed as well for any hikes and some bushwhack trips—do keep in mind that a mile on a hiking trail will seem a lot tougher than a mile on the treadmill! Some of the more remote scenic areas have no trails of any kind in them and it is possible to spend many days bushwhacking around. On the other end of the scale are many terrific views and photo opportunities waiting for you right along an easy path.

GPS. Seems like everyone out in the woods is using a GPS unit these days. While I do find them handy from time to time, it is best not to rely on them for your normal navigation. Sometimes they are great and will help you find a specific location that is not on a trail or road. I have included GPS coordinates in the text for many remote locations and special features along the trails. All coordinates use UTM NAD 27, Zone 15S. And if you are not a GPS junkie, sorry to clutter up this guidebook with all the numbers! By the way, here is one of my most favorite locations in the state—the largest living thing in Arkansas—which is very easy to find if you have the GPS coordinates (UTM 674415E, 3791094N).

MAPS. We have tried to produce original maps that accurately show the features that are most important for each of the scenic areas. We used a variety of sources as the base maps, including topos, park brochures, planning maps, highway maps, and some computer software maps. We combined this data with our own on site experience and created the maps using a computer drawing program and pen and tablet. There is a legend inside the back cover that shows the symbols for all maps, however you won't find a scale since that varies from map to map. Some of the maps will give you all the info that you need while others are designed to get you to an area where you can then obtain current park brochures with more detailed info.

PHOTOGRAPHY TIPS. I took all of the photographs in this guidebook (actually the one on page 157 is a little suspect), most of them in the past couple of years. Photography is all about light, and your best photos will happen when you have great light. Early and late in the day is the best light—avoid the harsh light of midday sunshine. Overcast days are great for outdoor photography too. Steady your camera, get the exposure correct, and shoot LOTS of pictures! Wildlife photography is difficult at best—get close to your subject, then wait to take the photo until your subject stops moving to avoid a blurry animal (oops you can see from page 157 that I missed that tip!). If your subject is brighter than the background it will stand out more. And finally, attend a photo workshop—I have workshops for beginners, intermediate, and advanced photographers throughout the year—see my web page for the latest schedule—**www.TimErnst.com**

ROADS. We have a variety of roads in Arkansas from the best interstates to the worst jeep roads. All of the roads noted in this guidebook can be traveled with a normal passenger vehicle, although jeep roads usually require high-clearance and/or 4wd vehicles. The rougher roads are marked as dashed-lines, while normal gravel roads are solid white and paved roads are solid black. Scenic drive roads will be solid red. Some roads have more than one name. In fact some have three or even four different names and numbers. We have tried to use the most common and current road names and numbers in the text and on the maps, however those are subject to change at the whim of the government. In order to save space and ink we have shortened "Forest Road" to FR and "County Road" to CR as in FR#1003 or CR#28. Most directions to remote locations will include specific mileages and it is best to zero your odometer and follow the directions. The mileages noted are often given in tenths, but keep in mind that these readings can vary from vehicle to vehicle, and will depend on such factors as tire wear, road conditions and driving habits. So just like the road numbers, you should use the mileage figures as your guide, but be aware that they may differ a little bit from what is listed here. The maps/directions are from local points—be sure to bring a state highway map too!

TRAILHEAD PARKING AREAS. Sometimes there are large, paved and well-marked trailheads to park at. Often there is no place to park at all, other than just a wide spot in the road. The main parking areas that are described in this book are indicated with a red "P" symbol while other parking areas are marked with a black "P" symbol. It is best to follow the mileage and turn directions in the guidebook instead of relying on parking areas being signed. People ask me all the time if their car will be safe at these parking areas. The simple answer is, who knows? In reality your car is probably just as safe at any remote parking area as it is parked in your front yard, however a break-in can happen anytime and anyplace. None of these parking areas that I know of are 100% secure, so play it safe and hide your valuables or leave them at home.

SYMBOLS. Here is the list of symbols that appear above each map that can be used for a quick visual reference about the scenic area:

🚶	Hiking trail	🛶	Canoe trail or boat access
🚗	Scenic drive	🦇	Caving, wild or commercial
👁	Wildlife watching	⛺	Campground or camping available
🐕	Dogs allowed on leash	ℹ	Visitor Center
♿	Wheelchair accessible	$	Entrance fee required

RESOURCES. There are many great publications available that will give you more information about these and other scenic areas in Arkansas, plus there are literally millions of web pages online that are updated with fresh info. There is a web page address listed on each map in this book that is always a good place to start. You can also check the "outdoor links" section at **www.HikeArkansas.com** for links to most of the outdoor clubs and agencies in Arkansas. And you can find a lot more detailed info about scenic areas, hiking trails, waterfalls, wildlife areas, and scenic drives in the following guidebooks:

Arkansas Dayhikes for kids guidebook, *Arkansas Hiking Trails* guidebook, *Arkansas Waterfalls* guidebook, and *Buffalo River Hiking Trails* (all by me); plus *Arkansas Watchable Wildlife* guidebook by the Arkansas Game and Fish Commission, and *Scenic Driving the Ozarks* by Don Kurz.

OK, that should get you started. It has taken me many years to put this list of my favorite scenic locations together, and I hope you enjoy visiting them as much as I did doing the research! Come to think of it, I do believe there are a few of these places that I need to return to and take more pictures, so I suspect you may see me out there. Good luck, be safe, and have a great time exploring the best of Arkansas!

See ya in the woods, in the prairies, and in the swamps!

Tim Ernst

Ozarks Region

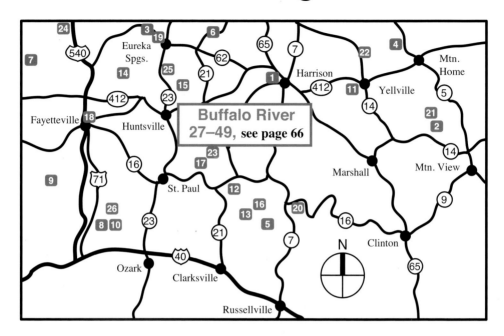

The OZARKS REGION by its very geological nature contains many great scenic natural features from tall sandstone and limestone bluffs to thundering waterfalls and meandering streams filled with moss-covered boulders. The vegetation is lush in the deep forests where you can find carpets of colorful wildflowers under towering oak trees. Flowering dogwoods, redbuds, and umbrella magnolias—oh my! The wilderness comes alive in the springtime and there is no other area in the country that can match our blooming display. Our fall color season is legendary, with the hardwoods blazing for weeks. There are scenic views that look out over vast expanses of rolling ridges, and intimate landscapes that draw you in. And there are wild critters galore including a healthy population of black bears and a growing herd of elk that contains some prize bulls as grand as you'd see anyplace in the country. There are natural wonders underground too and we have many commercial and wild caves for you to explore.

There are, in fact, so many great places to visit in the Ozarks that I have split up this section into two—one being the Ozarks in general, which we will cover in this section, and the other being just the Buffalo River drainage, which begins on page 66. Since I have spent my entire life living in the Ozarks, these are the places that I know best, and also the ones I return to with my camera in hand over and over again. Some of them are pretty tough to get into and require a bit of backcountry skill, while others can be seen from a short hike or even right from your car.

Scenic Areas in the Ozarks Region

1

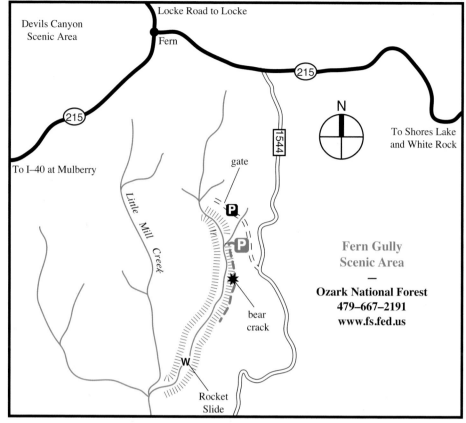

FERN GULLY SCENIC AREA has been hiding just out of sight forever, but recently it has been discovered by kayakers and rock climbers and has turned out to be one of the very best little scenic areas in all of the Ozarks (and given "special interest area" protection by the forest service—thanks!). It is very easy to get to, and you can visit some parts of it with little effort, or spend an entire day bushwhacking through difficult terrain. Basically this area is a steep drainage where the creek runs down through a boulder-strewn paradise (great for kayakers when the water is high), and it is rimmed with tall sandstone bluffs which provide endless areas of exploration both below and on top of the bluffs. You'll find many interesting bluff "features," like house-sized chunks that have broken off from the main bluffline just sitting in the middle of the forest; and at least one area where the bluff has split apart and you can walk right on up through it. There are tons of azalea bushes that light up the place in April, and of course, lots of ferns! There is a pretty nice waterfall downstream a ways too (named the "Rocket Slide" by kayakers). At the moment there are no official hiking trails, but there are many well-worn paths created by rock climbers that will get you started.

From the primitive parking area take the path to the west and it will go a short distance over to the edge of the bluffline (UTM 408781E, 3941781N)—there is a spot to get down through the bluff and to the creek. You can explore below from that point downstream (to the left), or continue on top of the bluff along the path on over to a "bear crack" in the bluffline (UTM 408759E, 3941552N) and beyond. The waterfall is located nearly a mile downstream (UTM 408313E, 3940595N) and requires a pretty serious bushwhack to get to (lots of great scenic stuff along the way, but it is a tough bushwhack). Below

The Rocket Slide gives kayakers quite a thrill during high water (above) ; a "bear crack" leads up through the bluffline (right)

the falls the creek eventually runs into Little Mill Creek, and that is the end of the really neat stuff.

Fern Gully is located northeast of Ft. Smith near the community of Fern (and right next door to Devils Canyon, and on the way to White Rock Mountain). To get to the parking area take the Mulberry exit on I-40 (#24) and go north on Hwy. 215 to the community of Fern. Go .7 mile past the sharp turn there and TURN RIGHT onto FR#1544 (gravel). Go 1.6 miles and TURN RIGHT onto a little logging road and go SHARP RIGHT (don't take the little road that goes straight ahead here). Go .2 mile and pull into a parking area on the left—if you keep going the road is gated at another parking area.

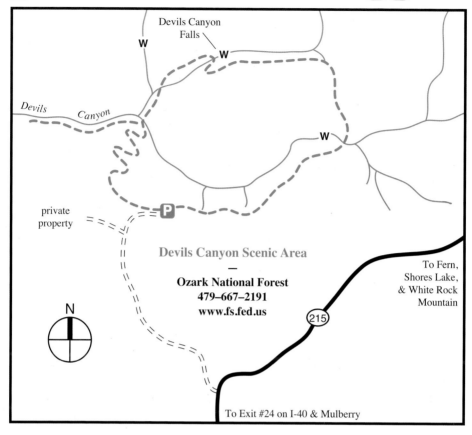

DEVILS CANYON SCENIC AREA, near Fern, is a tough place to get in and out of, but there is a spectacular 63' tall waterfall (UTM 406317E, 3944036N) and lots of other neat stuff to see if you are up for some difficult bushwhacking. The parking area is at the edge of the canyon, and you simply pick your way down into the canyon and then explore around. The map shows a "route" over to the waterfall that I normally use, which is to hike around the top of the rim on the old road, cross the creek, then head over to the next drainage and follow it on down to the big waterfall. You can scramble down below the falls and have a look around, then continue downstream where two creeks will come together. There is some nice exploring to do up the other creek too, but you should reserve some time to explore downstream as well and visit the big bluffs and other interesting features along the creek. Then it is a tough hand-over-fist bushwhack back out to the top of the rim. If you are still alive after this trip and have the time, be sure to visit Fern Gully that is almost right next door (see previous pages).

Take the Mulberry/Hwy. 215 exit (#24) off I-40 east of Ft. Smith and head north on Hwy. 215 to the tiny community of Fern. Zero your odometer there and head back south of Fern on Hwy. 215—go 1.4 miles and TURN RIGHT (west) onto an unmarked dirt road. A truck or 4wd vehicle helps as this road gets a little bit rough. Follow the road up and over a small hill—STAY STRAIGHT at the intersection (the left fork goes into private property)—and PARK once you come to the edge of the canyon .6 mile from the highway.

Devils Canyon Falls is the tallest of several waterfalls in this scenic area

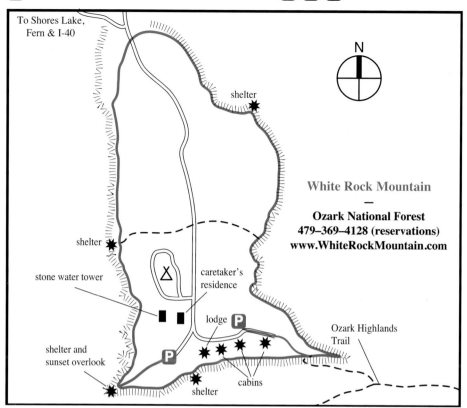

WHITE ROCK MOUNTAIN has the best sunset view in the Ozarks. As the sun sinks into the mountains you can see layers upon layers of forested ridges going all the way to Oklahoma. This small mountaintop is rimmed with sandstone bluffs, and you can hike the easy two-mile trail all the way around the top of the bluffs and get terrific views the entire way. Sunrise is great too, and holy cow, the fall colors can be just incredible! There is a forest service campground and picnic area up on top plus three rustic stone cabins and a lodge building for larger groups that are available for rent year-round. Folks have been coming up to White Rock for the views and to stay in the cabins for many generations. The recreation area and cabins were built by the CCCs in the 1930s and when the government threatened to tear them all down we stepped in and formed the Friends of White Rock and were able to restore the cabins and lodge and get them back up and running once again. There are also four CCC-built pavilions located along the bluff and the original stone water tower is located right behind the caretaker's house. When the CCCs built something, it was intended to last a long time. You can also access the Ozark Highlands Trail and the loop trail down to Shores Lake from the far end of the mountain.

The cabins fill up quickly on weekends, so plan far ahead, especially for fall or springtime visits. One of the very best times to be snug in a cabin is during the winter months, although be prepared for some really "rustic" living—there is no phone, tv, or central air—heat is provided by you keeping the fireplace going, although the caretaker will provide plenty of firewood! One reason the cabins remain rented far in advance is because folks keep coming back for years and years—the sign of a very special place.

There are many ways to get up to White Rock, but the easiest is to take the Mulberry exit off of I-40 (#24) and head north on Hwy. 215 for 3.0 miles past Fern and

Fall color along the western rim of White Rock Mountain

TURN LEFT onto paved FR#1505 (Shores Lake Road). Take this road past Shores Lake where it will turn to gravel and become Bliss Ridge Road. Continue 4.0 miles and TURN LEFT onto FR#1003 (White Rock Mtn. Road). Go 2.2 miles and TURN RIGHT onto Hurricane Road. And finally go to the top of the hill, TURN RIGHT and go past the neat White Rock stone entrance and it will end at the cabins—the great sunset lookout will be to the right of the lodge at the picnic area (UTM 413342E, 3949611N).

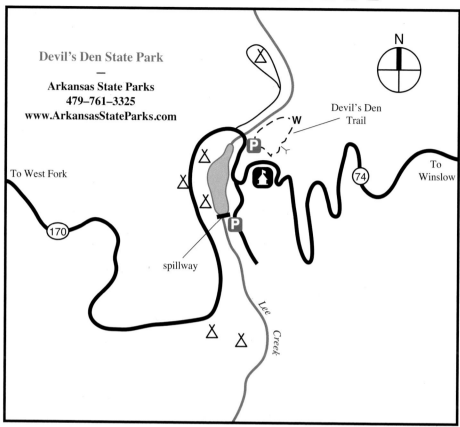

DEVIL'S DEN STATE PARK is one of the great family parks in the state with easy hiking trails, swimming pool, lake with paddle boats and fishing, picnic area, and dozens of rustic cabins, as well as several campgrounds. I love the spillway at the lake, and even though it is man-made, it was done so in such a way that it is quite beautiful. There is also a great natural waterfall, Twin Falls, that is the only one I know of in Arkansas where there is a walking trail bridge in the middle of the falls. And one of the main attractions of this park is also along that same trail, the trail to Devil's Den. This wild cave (which is actually a "crevice" or crack in the sandstone layers) has introduced countless would-be spelunkers to the joys of caving, and is a place you can take your kids into without having a lot of wild cave experience or special equipment (it is still possible to get lost or injured while in the cave though, so be careful!). There is a lessor-known limestone cave at the park too, Farmer's Cave, that requires a permit to explore—ask at the visitor center for the details. There is also the great 14-mile Butterfield Backpacking Trail that loops from the park and back again. There are a series of horse and mountain bike trails at the park also. Your first stop should always be the visitor center to get the latest info on the trails and the cave, and to pick up a park brochure.

     To get to the park from I-540 between Fayetteville and Ft. Smith, either take the Winslow exit (#45) and follow Hwy. 74 to the park, or take the West Fork exit (#53) and follow Hwy. 170 to the park.

*Twin Falls (left);
the spillway (below)*

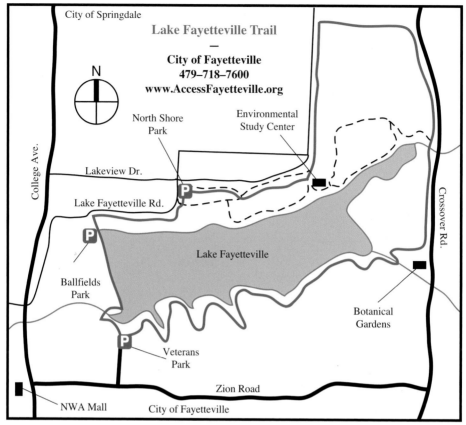

Lake Fayetteville Trail
—
**City of Fayetteville
479–718–7600
www.AccessFayetteville.org**

LAKE FAYETTEVILLE TRAIL. If you live in the area this is the place to go for a quick get-away out into the woods and away from the traffic and city life. It has long been a great fishing lake, but now there is a 5.3 mile trail that goes all around the lake that is prefect for hiking, jogging, and biking. There are lots of ducks and geese that use the lake, plus tons of other bird life. And if you are an early bird yourself, you can see a great sunrise from the dam—the photo at right was my first telephone book cover many years ago.

    The lake is located northeast of the Northwest Arkansas Mall—one trailhead is located just off of Zion Road right across from the mall behind Lowes (go east on Zion road .3 mile and TURN LEFT into Veterans Memorial Park—the gates are open from daylight until dark). A second trailhead is located at the ballfields in front of the dam (go north .4 mile from the mall and TURN RIGHT on Lake Fayetteville Road and head back behind the ball fields). And a third trailhead is located at North Shore Park—continue past the ball fields and the road will end at the park (great family park with a maze of trails).

    The trail is paved part of the way (from the Environmental Study Center to North Shore Park, and along the top of the dam to Veterans Park), including across a monster of a bridge over the spillway that takes the paved trail on to Veterans Park. The rest of the trail is a dirt path that winds around the shoreline of the lake, passing through the developing Botanical Gardens and forested areas along the way. It also passes the Lake Fayetteville Environmental Center, a great facility where our local kids spend some of their elementary school time (there is a side trail behind the center that follows the lakeshore back into the cove—a great waterfowl watching spot!). No swimming is allowed in the lake but the fishing is great.

A moment just before sunrise along the trail on top of the dam

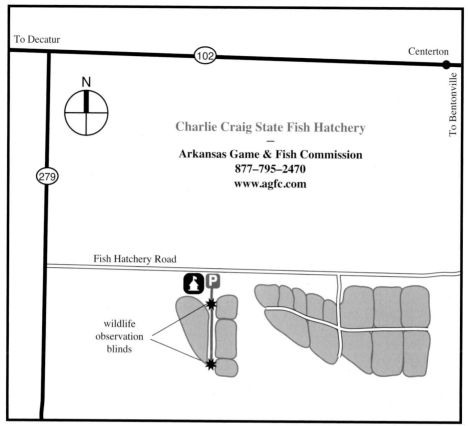

CHARLIE CRAIG STATE FISH HATCHERY is located in the extreme northwest part of the state and is one of the best places that I know of to view water birds of all types. The main area consists of several ponds with wildlife observation blinds that are accessible via a short foot trail from the parking area. These are great when there are active birds there. But when those ponds are dry or inactive, I like to drive on down to the much larger area of the hatchery, where you will find many more ponds (they raise catfish, crappie, bluegills and sunfish, walleyes, and bass). There is no trail here though, you simply drive around on the hatchery roads that go in between the ponds and look for birds. The activity really gets going when they draw down a pond or two—sometimes the birds come flocking in and it can be quite a display! There is a small visitor center on site and it is always best to stop by and ask them what birds are active, or even give them a call before you visit and see what is going on. Be sure to bring binoculars!

To reach the hatchery, take the Hwy. 102 exit on I-540 at Bentonville and head west to Centerton. Continue for another mile and then TURN LEFT onto Hwy. 279. Go .5 mile and TURN LEFT onto Fish Hatchery Road and then go .4 mile and TURN RIGHT into the hatchery parking lot. To reach the lower ponds, continue on another 1.4 mile and TURN RIGHT and drive into the pond area (the gates will be closed at night).

Canada geese and goslings on one of the nursery ponds

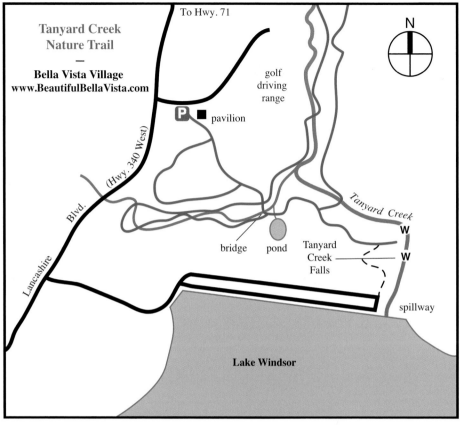

TANYARD CREEK NATURE TRAIL is a wonderful, easy loop trail right in the middle of Bella Vista. It was built and is maintained by volunteers, who have also posted at least 100 little signs along the way that tell all sorts of interesting details about things you will see, including identifying the many wildflowers that explode with color along the trail in the springtime. You can make a quick 30-minute hike to a neat waterfall and back, or spend half a day on this trail reading all of the signs. It is a "dog-friendly" trail, and they even have a special dog-watering station. My favorite time of the year for this trail is April or May when the flowers are in full boom and the waterfall is running. It is also a great trail at any time when you want to get out and hike around a little bit and not have to worry about ticks and chiggers or being out in the middle of the wilderness—you will have lots of friendly company.

      To get to the trailhead, head north on Hwy. 71 in Bella Vista and take the Hwy. 340/Town Center exit, then TURN LEFT. Go just about a mile on Hwy. 340/Lancashire Blvd. and TURN LEFT —it is signed as "Tanyard Creek Recreation." Then TURN RIGHT into the parking lot. There is an open pavilion there, and restrooms.

Tanyard Creek Falls (above); bloodroot wildflower (below)

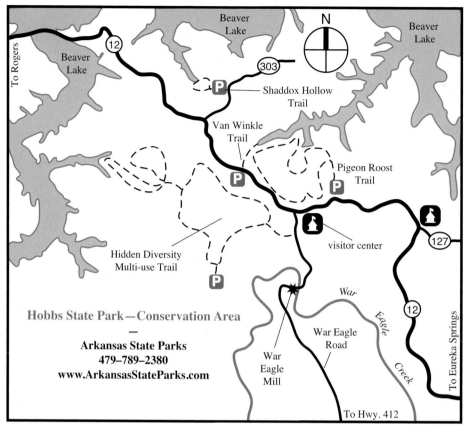

HOBBS STATE PARK-CONSERVATION AREA is located east of Rogers along Hwy. 12 and contains a variety of outdoor recreational opportunities including hunting, fishing, hiking, and horseback and mountain bike riding. The park is jointly managed by State Parks, Natural Heritage Commission, and Game and Fish Commission. This is the only state park in Arkansas that is open to hunting. There are some neat hiking trails in the park, including the short Shaddox Hollow Trail and historical Van Winkle Trail; plus a couple of longer trails including the 8-mile Pigeon Roost Backpacking Trail (camping is allowed), and the 16-mile Hidden Diversity Multiuse Trail for horses and bikes. Unfortunately, the trails are closed during hunting seasons—bummer. A lot of bald eagles hang around the lake in the wintertime, and you have a good chance of spotting one from the Pigeon Roost Trail.

The big, new visitor center at the park has some creative and educational exhibits and programs both inside and out. Plus there will be a very unique mock cave environment that you'll be able to enter by descending in an elevator into a lower level—really cool! Check their website for progress on the visitor center. This will be *the* outdoor fun and educational spot for kids and adults alike!

The park is located ten miles east of Rogers on Hwy. 12. Before you visit, you might want to check and see what the volunteer organization that cares for this park is up to—find out about their latest activities at www.FriendsOfHobbs.com.

White-tailed deer

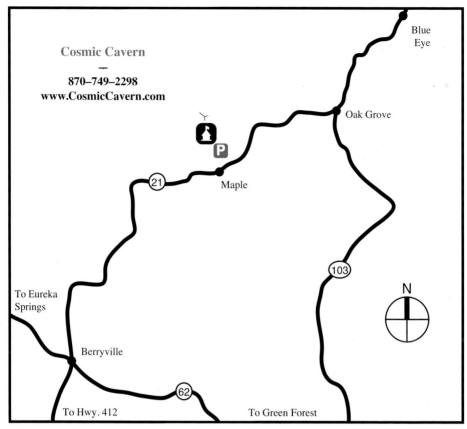

COSMIC CAVERN just north of Berryville is one of three commercial caves in this book, and is one of the most interesting of them all since it contains a couple of deep underground lakes that are seldom found on commercial cave tours. This cave is small when compared to Blanchard Springs Caverns, but it has a lot of colorful dripstone formations, those neat lakes, and makes a perfect cave for first-time visitors. If you want to experience a wild cave, they offer a wild cave tour that goes beyond the lighted tourist tour. NOTE: there is a narrow flight of steps at the beginning and end of all tours. They have a visitor center and gift shop, and gemstone panning and a fossil dig for the kids.

     To get to the cave take Hwy. 21 north out of Berryville 8.3 miles and the visitor center is on the left. The cave is normally open daily but check their web page or call if you are visiting during the off-season to be sure.

One of the deep lakes inside the cave

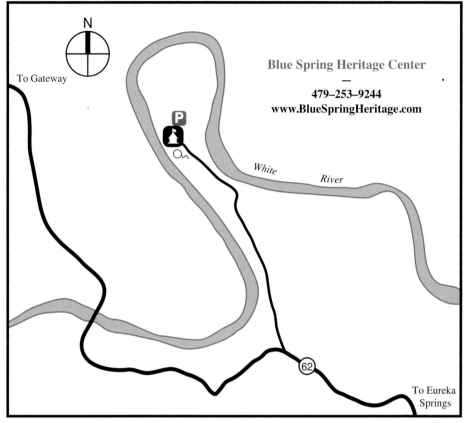

BLUE SPRING HERITAGE CENTER, outside of Eureka Springs, features the second largest spring in Arkansas—a giant blue pool of sparkling water that produces 38 million gallons a day. There are acres of landscaped hillside gardens and meadows, many of them covered with native wildflowers and other spectacular flowers, shrubs and flowering trees. This is a flower photographer's paradise! Lots of butterflies and birds too. There are historical features as well, including an old grist mill site from the 1800's, a stop on the Trail of Tears, and a bluff overhang that is on the national list of historic places. Much of the area is wheelchair accessible. There is a short free film that details much of the history of the area, and ask about the newest DVD being developed that includes footage from underwater scuba teams that dove deep into the spring!

To reach the center, go west from Eureka Springs on Hwy. 62 for 5.5 miles and TURN RIGHT at the big sign and go to the end of the road. There is an entrance fee, and they are closed in the winter (open from March 15th through Thanksgiving).

Blue Spring

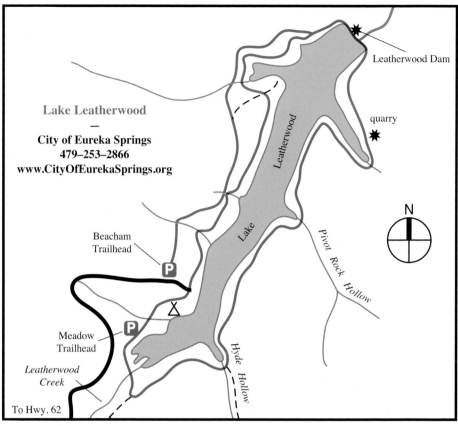

Lake Leatherwood
—
City of Eureka Springs
479–253–2866
www.CityOfEurekaSprings.org

Leatherwood Dam

quarry

Leatherwood

Lake

Pivot Rock Hollow

N

Beacham
Trailhead

Meadow
Trailhead

Leatherwood
Creek

To Hwy. 62

Hyde Hollow

LAKE LEATHERWOOD, at the edge of Eureka Springs, is a small mountain lake that fishermen have known about for years, but just recently is being discovered by other outdoor folks. There is a main hiking trail that circles the lake and goes across the dam that is made of cut limestone block, which at the time it was constructed in the 1930's was the largest one in the world of its kind. Lots of waterfowl use the lake, and you can find a ton of wildflowers along the trail and lakeshore in the early springtime. This is a very peaceful lake, especially once you get away from the main area that has camping, picnicking, swimming, and boat launch facilities. There are many other trails in the park too, most of them used heavily by mountain bikes.

      To reach the park, take Hwy. 62 west out of Eureka Springs, past the famous Thorncrown Chapel, and TURN RIGHT just past the entrance to the ballfields. The paved road ends at the lake. I normally start my hike at the far end of the recreation area to the right, and follow it counter-clockwise but you can hike it either direction and it will loop right back around to the parking area after the 3.7 miles. By the way, one time when I led a hike on this trail I met the most beautiful girl in the world—then we returned to the trail a few months later and got married! UPDATE—we just had our ten year anniversary (many said that would never happen), and we returned to Eureka Springs to hike this trail and then dine at Bubba's BBQ.

Lake Leatherwood (above);
looks like no skinny-dipping! (below)

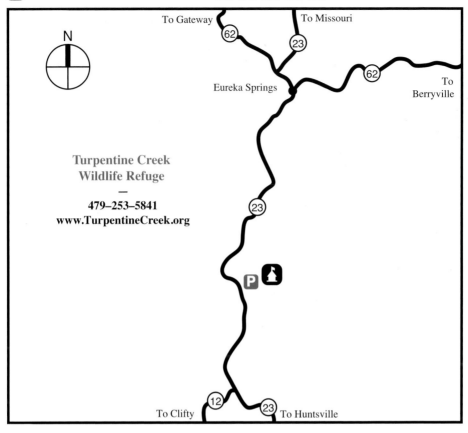

N

To Gateway   62

To Missouri   23

Eureka Springs

62

To Berryville

Turpentine Creek Wildlife Refuge
—
479–253–5841
www.TurpentineCreek.org

23

P

23

To Clifty   12

23   To Huntsville

TURPENTINE CREEK WILDLIFE REFUGE. Talk about lions, tigers, and bears—oh my! Not only is this an incredible story of a group of volunteers that slave away through the year to rescue abandoned, abused, and neglected big cats and other animals of many species, but the experience of visiting this refuge will have a profound effect on you. There are over 100 big cats here that you can visit up close and personal, including tigers, lions, and leopards; plus other species that are native to Arkansas like black bears, cougars, bobcats, and deer. The animals are simply beautiful, and you just cannot imagine not only the huge size of the lions and tigers, but especially the size of their PAWS! Even the native cougar paws would nearly cover up your entire hand. The refuge continues its work to place as many animals as possible into larger "habitats" and out of their cages to give them comfortable permanent homes. The staff (mostly volunteers) gives tours to see and teach about the animals, but if you ask around you will realize the majority of their time is spent simply taking care of the animals. And for a really special treat there are Bed and Breakfast rooms and a Treehouse available for rent right on the grounds—where else in this country can you look out the window and see tigers!

The refuge is located seven miles south of Eureka Springs on Hwy. 23 and is open all year but closed on Christmas day. There is an entrance fee that goes towards the upkeep of the animals and the grounds. Be sure to ask about adopting a big cat, bear or deer. And also check out their web page that contains photos and info about all of their big cats—get to know them even before you visit!

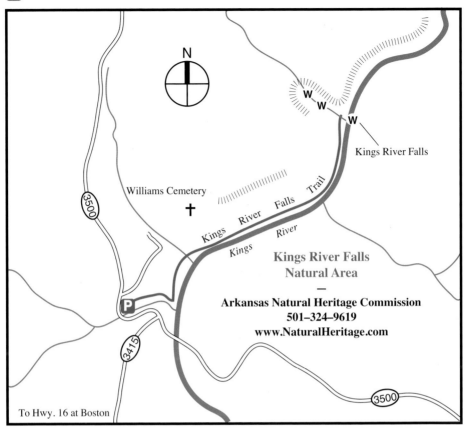

KINGS RIVER FALLS NATURAL AREA is one of those special places that I return to over and over again no matter what the season. The big waterfall is the main attraction (UTM 448178E, 3973011N), but I find myself exploring the side drainages and bluffs more and more each time I visit. The trail is easy, even for kids, and the pool below the falls is a good swimming hole in the summertime. Spring brings out many wildflowers along the trail, plus there are lots of wild azaleas and dogwoods blooming. There once stood a grist mill at the falls that utilized the force of the water to turn millstones that had been brought over from France (the mill had a fireplace and chimney and thus was known as the Chimney Mill). The mill was washed out by a flood in 1914. The Natural Heritage Commission now owns more land around the waterfall—looking downstream it is up on the bluffs to the left—so feel free to find a way up and explore, but be careful and don't fall!

To get to the trailhead go to the old community of Boston on Hwy. 16 between Pettigrew and Red Star (this is where the mighty White River begins). From Boston head north on CR#3175 (gravel) for 2.0 miles and TURN RIGHT at the fork onto CR#3415. Stay on this road 2.3 miles until you come to a "T" intersection—TURN LEFT onto CR#3500. Go a couple of hundred yards and park at the trailhead, which is located just across the bridge that goes across Mitchell Branch. (This trailhead was built in 2009—the old one next to the crumbling barn is no longer there.)

This is an easy, level trail (perfect for kids) that is marked with blue blazes. The trail begins at the parking area and heads downstream along the top of a small levy, and follows in between the creek (on the right) and hay field/fenceline (on the left). It comes

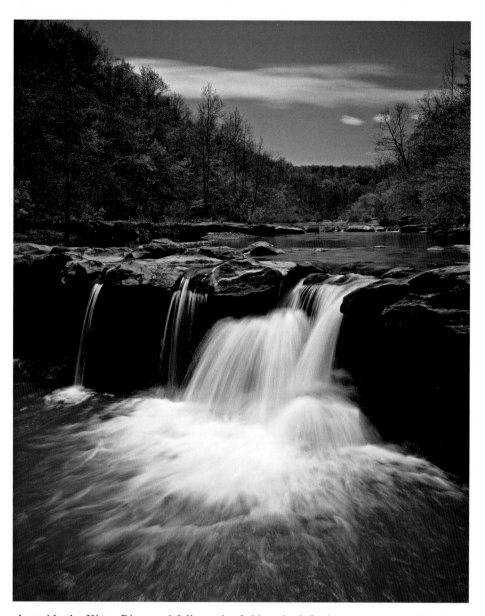

alongside the Kings River and follows the field to the left, then crosses a small stream. Parts of the old trail were washed away by the river so the trail was moved up onto the edge of the field here and continues downstream. There is an old rock wall part of the way that defines the hay field. Besides tons of wildflowers that carpet the area in the spring, there are lots of wild azaleas around too. Stay next to the river, and you'll eventually come to the Natural Area boundary sign—the wonderful waterfall and pool are just beyond at .85. There is a small side creek coming in from the left there that has some nice waterfalls once in a while. The immediate area of the big falls was once used as a grist mill site—can you spot the marks carved into the stone?

This area is pretty nice all around—plan to spend some time here! To return to the trailhead simply head back upstream the way that you came in.

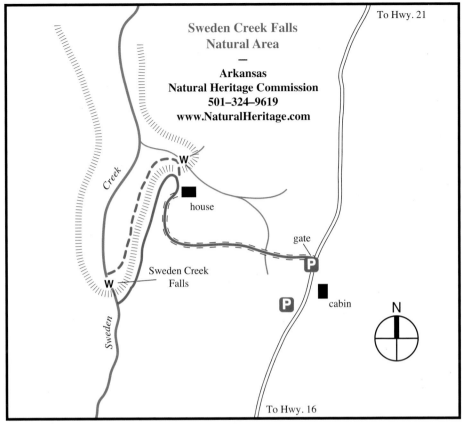

Sweden Creek Falls
Natural Area
—
Arkansas
Natural Heritage Commission
501–324–9619
www.NaturalHeritage.com

SWEDEN CREEK FALLS NATURAL AREA is a remarkable little scenic area with towering bluffs, wildflowers, ferns, and an 81' tall thundering waterfall as its focal point (UTM 458618E, 3980670N). The first half of the hike is down the road to an old house, but from there it is a bushwhack along the base of the big bluffs where the footing is often tricky. A new path now leads to the top of the falls for another incredible view.

The turnoff to get to the Natural Area is located on Hwy. 21 between Boxley and Kingston—from Kingston go 5.2 miles south on Hwy. 21 and TURN RIGHT onto the gravel road (hwy. sign may point to Red Star), or from Boxley go 3.9 miles north on Hwy. 21 and TURN LEFT onto the same gravel road. Stay on the gravel road for 3.1 miles, then PARK on the right. The road down to the old home place begins there, and will be gated. *NOTE: there is an alternate parking area just up the road on the road also—see map above.*

Hike down the old road trace .4 mile to the old home place. You will come to a garage first— VEER LEFT there and head down into the woods below the house following a marked path. There is a waterfall about 150 yards or so down there, and just to the left of it is a narrow corridor where you can get down through the bluffline* (red dotted line on map). Once you get to the bottom of the bluff TURN LEFT and follow along the base of the bluff. This bluff will curve back to the left and forms the eastern wall of the canyon. It will lead you right to the big waterfall at .9 mile.

*A path now leads to the left along the top of the bluff (solid red line on map), to the top of the waterfall (*dangerous bluff—be careful!!!*). You must return back to near the old home place since the bluff-top trail does not loop around.

Sweden Creek Falls

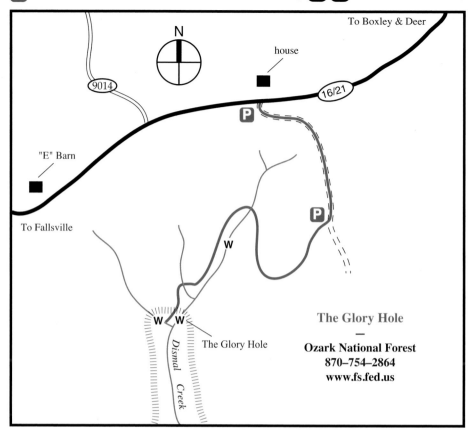

THE GLORY HOLE is one of the most interesting waterfalls in Arkansas. The creek has drilled a large hole right through the roof of an overhanging bluff, and the resulting waterfall pours out below (31' tall, UTM 464469E, 3964080N). The area around the falls is pretty nice too and includes towering bluffs, giant chunks of sandstone, and in the spring there are flowering magnolia trees that fill the little canyon with wilderness perfume!

To get to the spot to begin this hike, take Hwy. 16/21 east out of Fallsville for 5.7 miles. Here you will pass a red barn on the left that has a large, white "E" on the side of it. Go .5 mile past this barn, and pull off opposite a house that is up on the hill to the left. Park here on the shoulder—there isn't much room. (If you come to the Cassville Baptist Church, you've gone .7 of a mile too far. This pull-off is also 2.3 miles west of Edwards Junction.) If you have a 4wd you can drive down this jeep road another .25 mile and park.

From the highway hike along the jeep road about .25 mile, then TURN RIGHT at the bulletin board onto a lessor roadbed/trail that heads on down the hill. It gets a bit steep as it curves back to the right, and crosses the main stream at the bottom. Stay on this roadbed as it curves back to the left and heads down the hill, eventually turning into plain trail before landing on top of the bluffline. (There is a small waterfall or two upstream.) Be *extremely careful* if you make your way to the bottom! NOTE: there have been a couple of folks fall through the "hole" recently and were seriously hurt and had to be airlifted to the emergency room, so *please* don't go near the upper part of the falls!

The Glory Hole

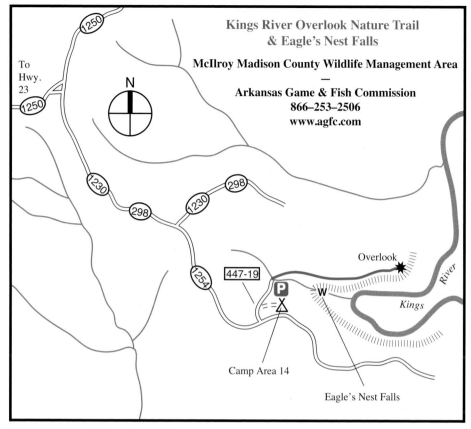

Kings River Overlook Nature Trail
& Eagle's Nest Falls

McIlroy Madison County Wildlife Management Area
—
Arkansas Game & Fish Commission
866–253–2506
www.agfc.com

To Hwy. 23

N

Overlook

447-19

P

W

Kings River

Camp Area 14

Eagle's Nest Falls

KINGS RIVER OVERLOOK NATURE TRAIL & EAGLE'S NEST FALLS is a short, easy hike on an old jeep road to a spectacular overlook of the Kings River in the McIlroy Madison County Wildlife Management Area. It is located between Huntsville and Eureka Springs off of Hwy. 23. From Forum go north 3.7 miles on Hwy. 23 and TURN RIGHT onto CR#1250 at the Management Area Sign (gravel); or from Eureka Springs head south on Hwy. 23 and go 4.2 miles *past* the Hwy. 12 intersection and TURN LEFT onto CR#1250. Go .1 mile and then follow signs to the trailhead (UTM 441117E, 4008786N). [From the highway go 3.1 miles on CR#1250 (CR#1425 joins it) and TURN RIGHT onto CR#1230/298. Go 1.0 miles and CONTINUE STRAIGHT onto CR#1254–Private Road (CR#1230 turns to the left there). Go another .7 miles and TURN LEFT onto management area road #447–19. Continue down the hill— *go past* Camp Area #14 for .3 to the big sign and gate and PARK on the right.]

From the parking area hike past the gate and sign on and old jeep road and go across a small stream. The road/trail curves to the right and remains mostly level. Continue on this route until you come to the very end of the road at .5, and then just off to your right will be the terrific overlook of the Kings River (UTM 441959E, 4008792N). *DANGER:* The overlook is at the edge of a tall bluff and there are no barriers—hold onto your kids all the time!

Eagle's Nest Falls (UTM 441292E, 4008786N) is located below the trail about 1/3 of the way in—you will notice a small bluff up to the LEFT of the jeep road, and then look for a beaten path *down to the RIGHT* of the jeep road at this poing and this will take you to the head of the waterfall not far away. (Not marked—see map above.)

Kings River Overlook (above); Eagle's Nest Falls (below)

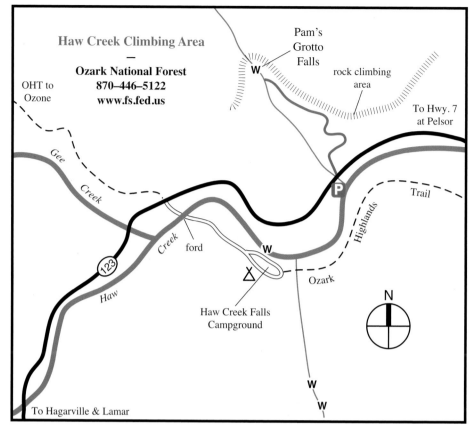

Haw Creek Climbing Area
—
Ozark National Forest
870–446–5122
www.fs.fed.us

OHT to Ozone

Pam's Grotto Falls

rock climbing area

To Hwy. 7 at Pelsor

Trail

Highlands

P

Ozark

ford

123

Haw Creek Falls Campground

Haw Creek

N

To Hagarville & Lamar

HAW CREEK CLIMBING AREA. I first stumbled onto this beautiful spot in 1982 while looking for a possible route for the Ozark Highlands Trail. I knew it was a very special place then. The next time I saw the 37' tall waterfall I was with my future bride, who the falls are now named after. We were working with a group of 60 volunteers from the Petra Rock Climbing Gym in Springfield, MO, and helped them build the short, but steep trail up to a rock climbing area. Climbers seem to know great scenery when they see it, or perhaps it is just that great climbing areas are often quite scenic! Either way the giant bluffs in this area are great, and of course, I am rather partial to the waterfall.

Take Hwy. 123 to Haw Creek Falls Campground (located between Lamar and Pelsor near the Big Piney River), then go .5 mile east on Hwy. 123 from the turnoff to the campground. There is a pulloff that drops down to a small parking area on the RIGHT— park there (you will be next to Haw Creek, UTM 477191E, 3948271N). The trail begins *across* the road and to the right of the small creek that comes out of the forest and goes under the highway.

Follow the trail up the hill about .25 mile to the base of the big bluffs. TURN LEFT and follow along the base of the bluffs and you will come right into the grotto after about .5 mile total. You will be hiking along, admiring the bluff, and all of a sudden there it will be! The waterfall itself is guarded by a house-sized boulder. It is a small area with a giant personality, and really looks good with a lot of water (UTM 476906E, 3948644N).

Pam's Grotto Falls

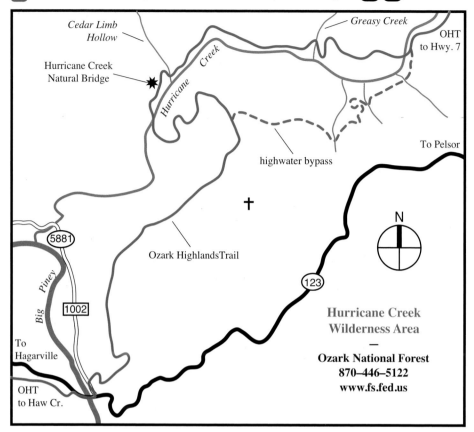

Cedar Limb
Hollow

Hurricane Creek
Natural Bridge

Hurricane Creek

Greasy Creek

OHT
to Hwy. 7

highwater bypass

To Pelsor

+

N

5881

Ozark HighlandsTrail

123

Big Piney

1002

To
Hagarville

OHT
to Haw Cr.

**Hurricane Creek
Wilderness Area
—
Ozark National Forest
870–446–5122
www.fs.fed.us**

HURRICANE CREEK WILDERNESS AREA. While you have more than 15,000 acres to explore here, the main route through this great wilderness area is the Ozark Highlands Trail that goes right through the middle of it. One of the main scenic features is the Hurricane Creek Natural Bridge (UTM 479763E, 3952593N), a sandstone arch that towers high above at the top of a beautiful painted bluff. The creek itself is just plain gorgeous, filled with emerald pools, whitewater, and a house-sized boulder or two strewn about just for fun. And in the summertime there is still plenty of water left over for a few swimming holes. In short, it is one of the most scenic parts of the 165-mile long Ozark Highlands Trail, and one of the best wilderness areas in the state.

It is a 19.5 mile backpack through the wilderness from the Big Piney Trailhead on Hwy. 123 (between Hagarville and Pelsor) to Fairview Campground on Hwy. 7 (just north of Pelsor). The heart of the really scenic stuff is six to seven miles in from Big Piney (you come to the natural bridge at 6.0), but you will enjoy all of the trail as it winds through the forested hillsides and along the creek. NOTE: the trail crosses Hurricane Creek twice, and if the water is high it can get dangerous—there is a "high water bypass" trail that avoids these crossings, but you also miss much of the best scenery. The ***Ozark Highlands Trail Guide*** is the best resource for info on this trail. Also note there is not much level ground to camp on so keep your group size small, six hikers or less is best.

The photo at right is a self-portrait taken with an old 4/5 camera outfit (weighed 60 pounds) that I used to haul around in my younger days. There is a "Natural Bridge" sign along the trail that will lead you to the bottom of the bluff where you can look up and see the bridge, but getting to the top is a much more difficult and dangerous task.

Hurricane Creek (above); on top of the natural bridge (below)

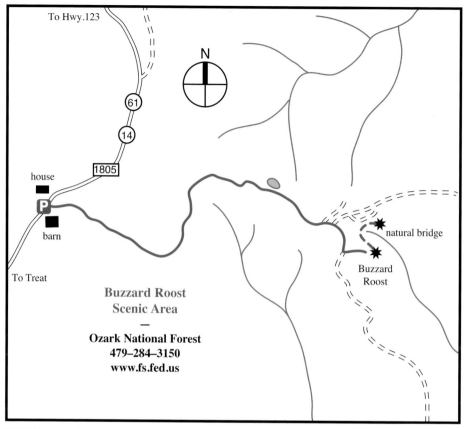

To Hwy.123

N

61

14

1805

house

P

barn

To Treat

natural bridge

Buzzard
Roost

**Buzzard Roost
Scenic Area**

—

**Ozark National Forest
479–284–3150
www.fs.fed.us**

BUZZARD ROOST SCENIC AREA has been around for a long time, but few folks knew where it was (until now). An easy hike along a four-wheeler trail takes you out to the top of a bluff (UTM 487934E, 3943122N) that is laced with weather-worn crevasses—some 40-50 feet deep—and a "turtle-rock" like sandstone cap. It is just, well, kind of a weird place, but *very* scenic. This big bluff area looks out across quite a view to the east, where you can get a great photo of the rising sun. Caution is advised for kids and adults in this area—a fall might be fatal. You can scramble down and get to the bottom of those crevasses (from the hillside behind you) and find some mighty neat stuff. There is a small sandstone arch around on the north side of the bluffs, but hold onto your hat—there is a GIANT sandstone arch/bridge nearby (UTM 487962E, 3943293N)—one of the largest and most impressive in Arkansas! You will have to bushwhack across a steep hillside to find this big arch—just follow the contour to the north at the same level from the little arch or top of the first bluff, across a small drainage, and then to the beginning of the next bluff—not recommended for everyone since this is a really steep scramble. The big arch is located 100 yards into the next bluffline. You can get down below the arch from the little drainage you cross or simply follow along the top of the bluff for the rooftop view.

      To reach this great scenic area, find your way to Pelsor on Hwy. 7 (between Jasper and Dover) and turn west onto Hwy. 123. Go 4.7 miles and TURN LEFT onto FR#1802/1805, CR#14/61 (gravel—this road has five names, also called Treat Road!). Go 6.5 miles on this road—there is a small white house on the right and an old barn on the left—park your car where you can along the road. The hike begins right in front of that old barn and heads into the woods. The first hundred feet or so are private property, but

Sunrise under the great arch on December 21st (above);
early morning from on top of Buzzard Roost (below)

then you will be on forest service land. Follow this four-wheeler road for 1.8 miles, past a little pond, and past another four-wheeler road that goes off to the left until you come to an intersection—TURN RIGHT and follow this four-wheeler road for a few hundred yards and it will curve around to the left and end at the top of the Buzzard Roost Bluffs area at 1.9 miles—scramble down the hillside ahead to the top of the bluffs.

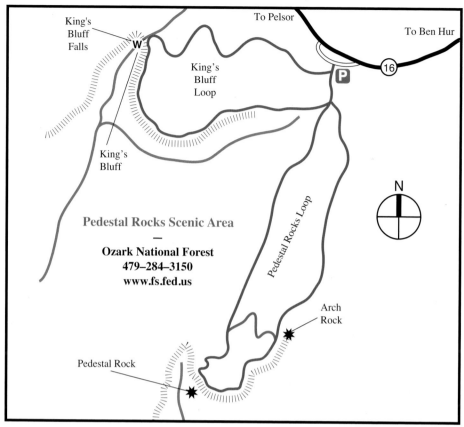

PEDESTAL ROCKS SCENIC AREA is really two areas in one—Pedestal Rocks and King's Bluff. Both have some unique weather-worn sandstone formations, and there are some really nice waterfalls too. Pedestal Rocks is the famous side of this double-loop trail. There are some great views of the "pedestals" and the countryside from on top of the bluff, but you can also get down below and find some really neat areas back inside the bluffs. There is a tall waterfall over on the King's Bluff side (114' tall—takes a lot of water to make it look great), and you can get down under the bluff there also and find several other really nice waterfalls. On the other end of King's Bluff there are more sandstone formations or "hoodoos" that have been carved out by Momma Nature over the years. Oh yes, and while you are down below the bluff looking at waterfalls, you can scramble around and play hide and seek with the many nooks and crannies, tunnels and overhangs under the bluffs to the south. Both trails are easy hiking.

     To get to the trailhead, take Hwy. 16 east from Pelsor on Hwy. 7 (Pelsor is located between Russellville and Jasper). Go about 6.0 miles and look for the sign to the RIGHT. If you get to Ben Hur, you've gone too far, so just turn around and go back about 2.5 miles. There is a picnic table and restroom at the trailhead, but camping is not allowed.

*Pedestal Rock (above);
sandstone "hoodoo" along
King's Bluff (left)*

53

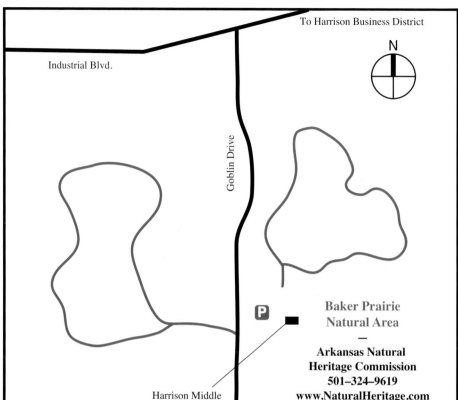

BAKER PRAIRIE NATURAL AREA is one of the smallest tracts in this book, but at the right time of the year it is indeed one of the most spectacular. The 70 acres are located right in the middle of Harrison, yet you can hike the mowed paths and be in the middle of wild prairie in just a few minutes. While spring and summer blooms can cover the landscape here (sometimes nearly solid coneflowers), there are five special wildflower species that grow here: Ozark wake robin, prairie violet, royal catchfly, downy gentian, and silky aster. You can also find several threatened animal species here, including: grasshopper sparrow, prairie mole cricket, and ornate box turtle. Like all of our prairies, the best way to view them is to get out and wander around. You will find plenty of neat things to look at.

The natural area is located across the street from and also to the north of the elementary school in Harrison on Goblin Drive. From the intersection of Hwy. 65/412 and 65B, go west on Industrial Blvd. .9 mile and TURN LEFT onto Goblin Drive and go .4 mile up the hill and park at the middle school on the left. There are two trails (actually just mowed paths through the prairie), one on each side of the road. The trail on the western side is .75 miles roundtrip and begins at the natural area sign. The trail on the eastern side is .75 miles as well (including the hike from the parking lot), is called the Dayle McCune Trail, and begins across the small field just to the north of the school. This prairie is actually owned and managed by both the Arkansas Natural Heritage Commission and The Nature Conservancy.

Pale purple coneflowers and crescent moon in June

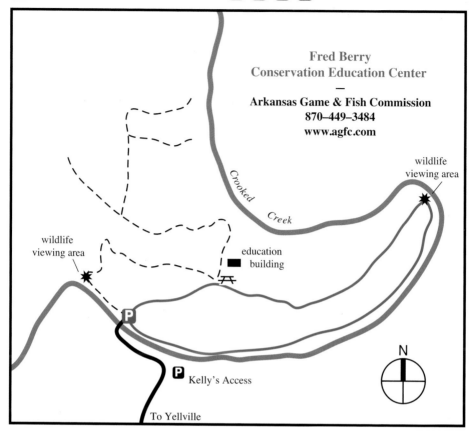

**Fred Berry
Conservation Education Center**
—
**Arkansas Game & Fish Commission
870–449–3484
www.agfc.com**

wildlife
viewing area

Crooked Creek

wildlife
viewing area

education
building

N

P

P Kelly's Access

To Yellville

FRED BERRY CONSERVATION EDUCATION CENTER, on Crooked Creek just outside of Yellville, is one of several great educational facilities operated by the Game and Fish Commission that provide some unique opportunities for local school students. This one just happens to be located right on Crooked Creek and has hiking trails, great floating and fishing, and meadows filled with wildflowers in the springtime. Oh, to be a kid again and be able to attend some of their classroom programs! They will be building more hiking trails in the future, but now have one that runs upstream along the banks of Crooked Creek where you can spot all sorts of birds and other wildlife. The money to fund these centers comes from "fine" money—the money from fines collected from game violators. If you are a teacher and want to find out about how your class can enjoy the benefits of this wonderful facility, just give them a call.

      To reach the center from Yellville, go to the west end of town on Hwy. 412 and TURN LEFT onto MC#4002 (across from the sheriff's office) and head towards Kelley's Access, then continue on across Crooked Creek and park in the lot just on the other side. The education center is located another half mile beyond, and while there are some nice native wildflowers along the way, the center is not operated as a visitor center and there may not be any staff available.

A meadow of larkspur wildflowers (above); baby skunks (below)

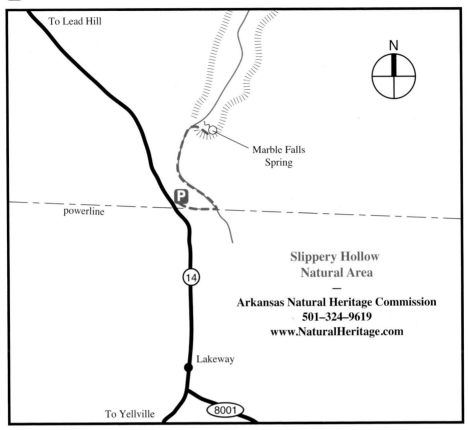

To Lead Hill

N

Marble Falls
Spring

P

powerline

14

**Slippery Hollow
Natural Area**
—
**Arkansas Natural Heritage Commission
501–324–9619
www.NaturalHeritage.com**

Lakeway

To Yellville   8001

SLIPPERY HOLLOW NATURAL AREA, just north of Yellville, is a secret spot that contains towering limestone bluffs, fern-covered hillsides, a cave system that is home to the endangered Ozark big-eared bat, and a beautiful spring that pours from the hillside over moss-covered rocks. This is a fragile and magical place that has never seen much use or visitation over the years. The main scenery is right around the spring area, which is not too far from the highway, but is located in a very steep ravine that is difficult to get in and out of and not recommended for the casual visitor—it is all bushwhacking, there is no trail. There is more to this place though that requires exploration—both down the little stream and along the base of the big bluff—but it is unforgiving landscape, and it is easy to slip and get hurt. Only visit this place in very small groups of two or three folks at a time, and tread lightly.

    To get to the natural area from Yellville, take Hwy. 14 north out of town to Lakeway, then go .7 mile to a large transmission line crossing the road—PARK along the road under this powerline. Bushwhack down the hill under the powerline until you reach the bottom of the first little hill, then TURN LEFT and follow the small stream downstream (it may be dry). After about a quarter mile you will have to climb down a small bluff that is across the stream—Marble Falls Spring (UTM 520854E, 4022848N) will be around the corner, up to the right and flowing into the stream below—TREAD LIGHTLY while around the spring! From that same little bluff, you can explore around on the left side of the stream and find the base of a big bluff.

Marble Falls Spring

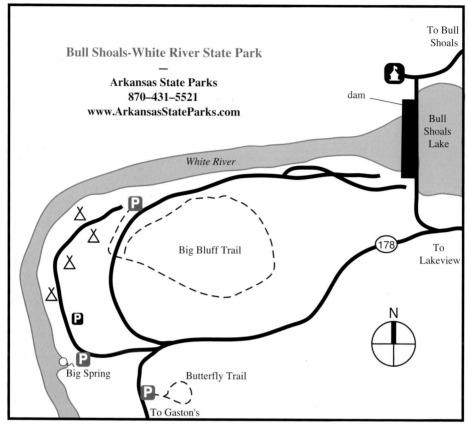

Bull Shoals-White River State Park
—
Arkansas State Parks
870–431–5521
www.ArkansasStateParks.com

BULL SHOALS-WHITE RIVER STATE PARK is a perfect place to go trout fishing, but you'll also find scores of great blue herons and other wildlife along the river, and in the early mornings a mist often rises from the cold waters that creates a spectacular sunlit landscape. There are hiking trails all over the place here, including one area that visits a special butterfly garden, and they have bluebird boxes throughout the park—the Bluebird Trail. There is a large spring that pours 29 million gallons of water a day into the river, and some of the best campsites right along the river you will ever see. Even though this park is often crowded with big RVs, as you hike around it feels more like a nature heaven than an RV park. Most of the park is located below Bull Shoals Dam, but there is a new giant visitor center up on top of the dam that overlooks the lake and is full of great educational exhibits and all sorts of other neat things to see and do—that should be your first stop.

To get to the park from Mountain Home, go six miles north on Hwy. 5, then TURN LEFT and go eight miles west on Hwy. 178—TURN LEFT before the dam to get to the camping area and hiking trails, or continue across the dam to get to the big visitor center. Or from Flippin simply take Hwy. 178 north for ten miles and you'll find the visitor center and the rest of the state park at the far end of town.

A pair of fishermen (above); bluebird and breakfast (left)

61

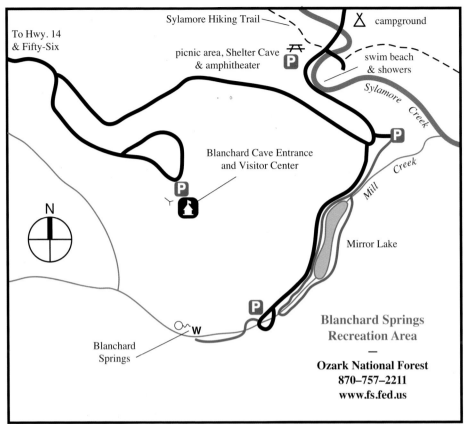

To Hwy. 14
& Fifty-Six

Sylamore Hiking Trail

△ campground

picnic area, Shelter Cave
& amphitheater
🅿

swim beach
& showers

Sylamore Creek

🅿

Blanchard Cave Entrance
and Visitor Center

🅿

Mill Creek

N

Mirror Lake

🅿

Blanchard
Springs

**Blanchard Springs
Recreation Area**
—
**Ozark National Forest
870–757–2211
www.fs.fed.us**

BLANCHARD SPRINGS RECREATION AREA is one of those places you will come back to many times—there is just something about it. Blanchard Springs itself would be enough, but then you add Mirror Lake and the historical grist mill just below it, the delightful waters of the North Sylamore Creek and the two swimming holes there, the natural bluff amphitheater and Shelter Cave next door too. All of these great natural features would be plenty to keep you busy for a while. But then you add one of the top commercial caves in the United States in Blanchard Caverns and you have one of the great nature lover spots in Arkansas. I worked at the cave for four summers when I was in college and came back nearly every weekend throughout the year just to play. If you are a cave lover, take both tours. For a real treat do the wild cave tour. Visit the springs and hike the trail around Mirror Lake and below the dam, then catch a trout or two for dinner. There is so much to see and do. And the 20-mile Sylamore Creek Backpacking Trail goes through the area too, so you can spend the weekend out in the woods if you like. One of my favorite things to do back in the 1970's (before there were any hiking trails) was to simply put on a pair of tennis shoes and wade upstream with a backpack on and spend the night wherever I happened to end the day. There is something really special about the water—I guess it is because it is filtered through all that limestone. Bring your kids and I bet they will return with theirs one day.

    The turnoff to Blanchard Springs is located just east of the community of Fifty-Six (between Big Flat and Sylamore on Hwy. 14). Everything is well marked, so just follow the signs to the cave, lake, spring, swimming areas, and campground.

Blanchard Springs (above); Mirror Lake spillway (below)

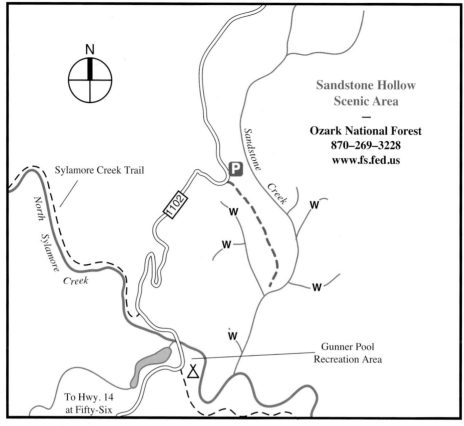

SANDSTONE HOLLOW SCENIC AREA is in a side canyon that feeds into North Sylamore Creek, just downstream from the Gunner Pool Campground. There is one major waterfall up in there, plus many others that spill over limestone bluffs past fern-covered hillsides. The little creek in the bottom of the hollow is full of life, color, and big trees towering over it. It is a wild and steep area that does not see many visitors—there is no trail, so you will be bushwhacking if you visit.

If you enter this area from Sylamore Creek, simply hike upstream and you'll find the big waterfall in the first little drainage to the left (UTM 571373E, 3983511N)—you'll see and hear it from the stream. The next left will take you deep into the scenic area where you'll find more waterfalls (UTM 571453E, 3983969N). Eventually the terrain gets too steep and you'll have to turn back. There are several other small drainages in the main stream that come in from the right side, and each one has a nice waterfall and cascades. There are blufflines and more streams and waterfalls to explore deeper into the natural area. When the water is high in Sylamore Creek, I drive up above the scenic area and park (no parking area, and not much room for a car—UTM 571302E, 3984587N), then follow a narrow ridgetop down to the creek—that route is marked on the map.

To get to Sandstone Hollow from the community of Fifty-Six, take Hwy. 14 west and TURN RIGHT onto FR#1102 at the sign and go 3.0 to the Gunner Pool Recreation Area (very nice camp spot). Continue on across the creek and climb up a series of switchbacks and PARK 1.4 miles from the bridge. You should see the narrow ridgetop off to your right—simply bushwhack down the top of that ridge and it will take you all the way down to the creek in the bottom (a long trip back out!).

Unnamed waterfall in the scenic area

Buffalo River Region

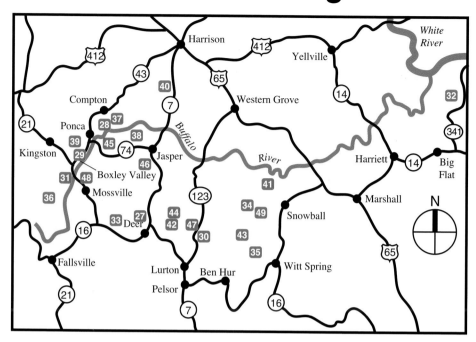

The BUFFALO RIVER REGION is the Yosemite of Arkansas—it is the most spectacular part of the state, the showcase, and folks have been drawn to it for centuries. There is just something about the water, and the quality of light that makes this area so special. The river itself became America's first National River in 1975, and while it has always been known as a premier floating stream, the drainage that creates it is filled with outstanding scenic features too, and we will visit many of them in this section of the guidebook.

There are towering bluffs, more waterfalls than you could visit in a lifetime, and lots of caves. Rock climbers flock to parts of this area for the great sandstone cliffs, and those cliffs just happen to be very scenic themselves, like the famous Sam's Throne, and the not-so-famous Cave Creek Bluffs and Owens-Ricketts Mountains areas. Besides the river park itself, there are several locations that have been set aside and protected for their great scenic qualities, including the brand new Smith Creek Scenic Area that is owned by the Nature Conservancy, Dismal Hollow Scenic Area in the national forest, and the king of wilderness areas in Arkansas, Richland Creek.

Scenic Areas in the Buffalo River Region

27

Map#	Page#	Name
27	86	Alum Cove Natural Bridge Scenic Area
28	104	Big Bluff and The Goat Trail
29	98	Boxley Valley Scenic Drive
30	82	Cave Creek Bluffs
31	96	Cave Mountain Cave
32	112	Dewey Canyon
33	90	Dismal Hollow Scenic Area
34	74	Dry Creek Scenic Area
35	68	Falling Water Scenic Drive
28	104	Goat Trail to Big Bluff
36	94	Hawksbill Crag
37	106	Hemmed-In Hollow
38	108	Indian Creek
39	100	Lost Valley
40	110	Mystic Caverns
41	78	The Nars and Skull Bluff
42	84	Owens Mountain Bluffs
43	70	Richland Creek Wilderness Area
		Twin Falls
		Sandstone Castle
44	84	Ricketts Mountain Bluffs
45	102	Roark Bluff
46	88	Round Top Mountain Trail
47	80	Sam's Throne
48	92	Smith Creek Scenic Area
49	76	Stack Rock

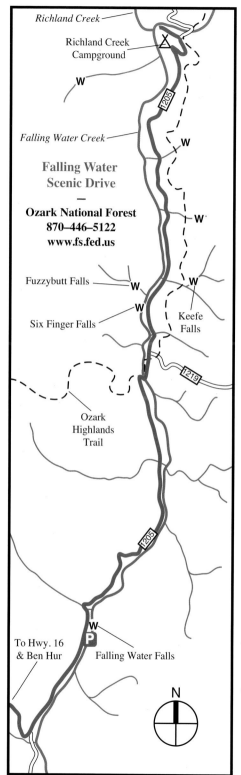

FALLING WATER SCENIC DRIVE visits not only the scenic border of the Richland Creek Wilderness Area, but several great waterfalls along Falling Water Creek, including the namesake waterfall that you can see right from the road (it's a good swimming hole too). At any point along the drive you can stop and get out and explore the creek's many cascades, emerald pools, and find views up and down the creek. When the water is up you are likely to see kayakers testing the whitewater. And the color in the fall is really nice, often reflecting in quiet pools along the drive. The 9.4-mile drive is all along a gravel forest road that is suitable for passenger cars (although sometimes when we have a flood the road can get slick). The drive follows Falling Water Creek and ends at Richland Creek Campground where Falling Water Creek joins with Richland Creek that flows out of the heart of the wilderness area. There is a nice swimming hole there too, as well as scenic views of the creeks and pools.

To reach this drive take Hwy. 16 east from Pelsor (located on Hwy. 7 between Jasper and Dover), past Pedestal Rocks Scenic Area, to Ben Hur. Continue past Ben Hur on Hwy. 16 for a mile and then TURN LEFT onto FR#1205/CR#68 (gravel). The best scenery will begin when you reach Falling Water Falls on the right at 2.3 miles (some great stuff just downstream along the creek, including large boulders, cascades and overhangs). Continue on the road to a bridge across the creek at 5.4 miles, and onto Six Finger Falls on the left at 6.0 miles (if you can get across the river there is a little side canyon just downstream that leads up to Fuzzybutt Falls), and finally turn into Richland Creek Campground at 9.4 miles. You can stop at just about any of the creeks that feed into Falling Water Creek along this route and bushwhack upstream and find a significant waterfall. The shortest way back to pavement is to turn around at the campground and return via the same route.

Falling Water Falls (above); Falling Water Creek in the fall (below)

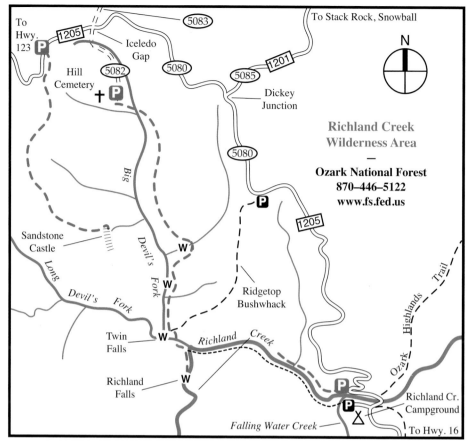

RICHLAND CREEK WILDERNESS AREA, TWIN FALLS, SANDSTONE CASTLE.

This is probably the most scenic of all our great wilderness areas, not only because of the famous waterfalls, but also because the creekbed is filled with smooth sandstone boulders and emerald pools, and there is something great to see at every turn. It is not a friendly place to hike through since there are no trails (the forest service is against them here), but with a map and some direction you can spend a day or a lifetime exploring this place and come back with many terrific memories and photos. I want to highlight three of the best locations here, but in between you will find plenty to explore and delight in. One is quite scenic and easy to get to, the second is the most famous yet difficult to get to, and the third is a "secret" spot that few people have ever been to.

One of my favorite photography locations in the state is along Richland Creek just upstream from the campground. There are boulders and pools and rapids one after another after another. It is a great location during all four seasons. To reach the trailhead, take Hwy. 16 east from Pelsor (located on Hwy. 7 between Jasper and Dover), past Pedestal Rocks Scenic Area, to Ben Hur. Continue past Ben Hur on Hwy. 16 for a mile and then TURN LEFT onto FR#1205/CR#68 (gravel). Continue on this road 9.4 miles (via the scenic drive on the previous pages) to Richland Creek Campground. You can drive into the campground if you like and see the swimming area, but we want to go past the entrance and over the bridge across the creek. Continue on the road around the curve, and up the hill to the next sharp curve and pull into the small wilderness access parking area. There is a trail that takes off from the back of this area and heads out level at first and then drops on down the hillside and comes alongside the creek in about a half mile—this is the beginning of the neat stuff on Richland Creek, and you simply get down to the creek and make your way as best you can upstream. The primitive trail continues on along the creek for a little ways but eventually disappears. You want to be down on the creek, in the creek, which means you should be getting wet and having a great time. NOTE: when the water is high this would be a dangerous place to be, so reserve this area for lower water levels. You can bushwhack up the creek as far as you like, and if you intend to spend the entire day, there is a path of sorts on the opposite side of the creek that goes upstream for a couple of miles that you could use to get to Twin Falls and to Richland Falls (UTM 503616E, 3961652N), but this is not recommended when the water is high—you would have to cross the flooded creek twice going in and out.

Here is one route into Twin Falls (UTM 503261E, 3962202N), which is one of the most scenic of all waterfalls in Arkansas, and you can do this even when water levels are very high since you don't have to wade the creek. By the way, there are several "twin falls" in Arkansas but this is the original and most famous one. There are two ways to get to the Hill Cemetery Trailhead—one is to drive from Richland Creek Campground on FR#1205/CR#5080 for 6.7 miles and then TURN LEFT at Iceledo Gap. Or take Hwy. 123 (paved) east out of Lurton (located on Hwy. 7 north of Pelsor and south of Cowell). Go 1.5 miles and TURN RIGHT onto FR#1200/CR#5070 (paved for the first mile). Go 6.8 miles and TURN RIGHT onto FR#1205/CR#5080. Go 1.6 miles and TURN RIGHT at the bottom of the hill—this is Iceledo Gap. Take this little road down the hill past a house and across a stream. It will end after .8 mile at Hill Cemetery. (The road is getting VERY bad—you need 4wd.)

Hike down the hill to the left of the cemetery on an old road trace that has been closed. It will cross Big Devil's Fork right away, then swing to the right and follow the creek downstream (the road is out in the woods and you don't see the creek). Stay on this old road until you get to a creek crossing and nice waterfall just below the road to the right at 1.8 miles. Now you have a couple of options. If you have a GPS or a good map you can continue on the road another .5 mile and then bushwhack down to Twin Falls,

Twin Falls

71

OR go the way that I do. I simply head down to the creek here and follow it downstream all the way to Twin Falls. There are several other waterfalls and lots of cascades along the way, but it is a difficult route. Either way the trip is about three miles one way.

Another route to Twin Falls is a bushwhack along a ridgetop, part way along an old road trace (none of this bushwhack is marked in the woods—see dotted black line on map). To reach this spot along FR#1205/CR#5080 go 1.0 miles south of Dickey Junction (or 3.9 miles north of Richland Creek Campground) and PARK at the old trace intersection on the south side of the road (UTM 504774E, 3964371N). Head out level into the woods along the old road trace, swing to the left/south, and follow the very top of the ridge *downhill* until you reach the bottom, then navigate over to Twin Falls.

The Sandstone Castle is a unique rock formation high up on the hillside that I first discovered while doing some photo work for the forest service back in the early 1980's (UTM 502416E, 3963626N). There are several rooms that have been carved out of the stone by wind, or water, or by the early architect of the earth. There is a giant stone pillar guarding the entrance to one series of rooms. This is a very strange and beautiful location. There is a tough way and an easy way to get up to the "Sandstone Castle in the Sky." Here is the tough way, but it is easy to find if you have a GPS. Along the way you used to see a pair of old millstones from a grist mill that disappeared long ago, but some stole them. First, follow directions to Twin Falls above, only instead of continuing all the way to the falls, simply bushwhack over to where the millstones used to be (UTM 503012E, 3963879N). Once you get to the small waterfall where the millstones used to be, simply bushwhack UP the little side creek (shown below) and you will run right into the Sandstone Castle at the top of the hill—it is a steep climb, but you can't miss the bluffs up on top. Once you have explored the castles, you can simply return to the trailhead via the same route; follow the bluffline to the end of the ridge and follow the ridgeline all the way down to the bottom, which ends at Twin Falls; or hike out the level way via the next description.

This is the easy way to the Sandstone Castle, but you need a GPS to find them

The historical millstones before someone stole them

Looking out from inside the Sandstone Castle

(UTM 502416E, 3963626N). If coming from Richland Creek Campground or Hill Cemetery, continue on FR#1205/CR#5080 up the hill from Iceledo Gap for .4 mile and park along the road where the last power pole is on the left side of the road. Or take Hwy. 123 (paved) east out of Lurton. Go 1.5 miles and TURN RIGHT onto FR#1200/CR#5070. Go 6.8 miles and TURN RIGHT onto FR#1205/CR#5080. Go 1.1 miles and PARK on the side of the road next to the last power pole on the right. You will see an old road heading out uphill into the woods going to the southeast here—that is your trail.

This old road will take you along a couple miles of ridgetops, past an old homesite, and runs mostly level with just a little bit of up and downing. Once you get towards the far end of the big ridge, you will veer off to the left edge and find the Sandstone Castle there. It is a great view out into the wilderness from the top, but you certainly want to find your way down to the bottom of the bluff and explore around inside the Castle. From that point, you can continue to follow the ridgeline as it drops steeply down the hill and ends right at Twin Falls, then you could hike back out to Hill Cemetery and then back up the forest road to your car. Or, from the Castle you could follow the little drainage down in front of the bluff all the way down to the pair of millstones at the bottom, then cross Devil's Fork and pick up the old road and take it back to Hill Cemetery. ALL of this is pretty difficult bushwhacking, and nearly impossible if you don't have a GPS. I recommend making this hike in the winter or early spring when the leaves are off the trees.

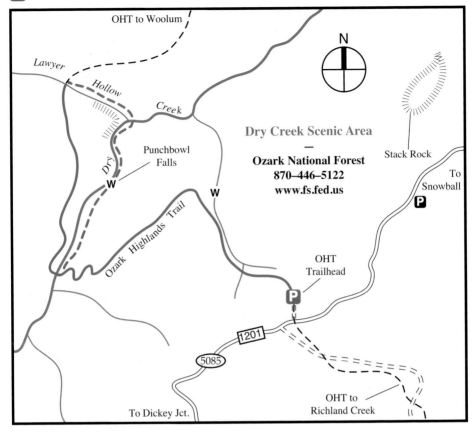

DRY CREEK SCENIC AREA. This is a beautiful scenic area that you must hike into along a trail and then do some pretty serious bushwhacking, but if you are tough enough it will be worth every step of the way. The Ozark Highlands Trail (OHT) takes you deep into the woods and past an old homesite and waterfall, then drops down a steep hillside to Dry Creek, where you will follow the creek downstream all the way to what I consider to be one of the most beautiful waterfalls in Arkansas—Punchbowl Falls (UTM 505380E, 3969964N). If you have a GPS you can follow a four-wheeler trail part of the way and then cut down to the falls. Once you have had your fill of the falls (if ever), continue to bushwhack downstream through a boulder-strewn paradise with giant sandstone blocks, thick walls of ferns, and thundering cascades. You will eventually come to the entrance to Lawyer Hollow that comes in from the left (UTM 505516E, 3970570N). There is a bluff face there that reminds me of the great El Capitan in Yosemite, and its face beams out into the wilderness. You want to make the scramble beneath this towering bluff and up into Lawyer Hollow, leaving Dry Creek behind. When you reach the point where the Ozark Highlands Trail crosses Lawyer Hollow, TURN LEFT on the trail and hike it all the way back to the trailhead (or you could continue on to the end of the OHT at Woolum). Sometimes I will backpack the trail to Lawyer Hollow and set up camp, then dayhike down to the creek and upstream to the big waterfall, then bushwhack back to camp. However you do it, this little section of heaven will give you plenty to explore. Watch for bears!

Take Hwy. 123 (paved) east out of Lurton (located on Hwy. 7 north of Pelsor and south of Cowell). Go 1.5 miles and TURN RIGHT onto FR#1200/CR#5070. Go 6.8

Punchbowl Falls

miles and TURN RIGHT onto FR#1205/CR#5080. Go 3.4 miles to Dickey Junction and
TURN LEFT onto FR#1201/CR#5085. Go 3.0 miles and TURN LEFT into the trailhead
and PARK. The trail heads out down the road and then TURNS LEFT off of the road and
into the woods after only a couple hundred feet. Follow this trail on down to Dry Creek,
then begin your bushwhack downstream.

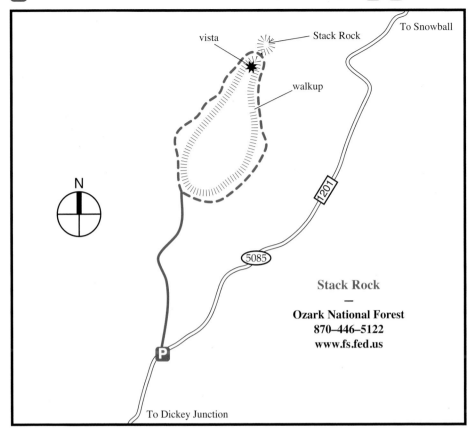

To Snowball

vista — Stack Rock

walkup

N

1201

5085

Stack Rock
—
Ozark National Forest
870–446–5122
www.fs.fed.us

P

To Dickey Junction

STACK ROCK is a narrow mountaintop, completely rimmed with tall bluffs, that has recently been discovered by rock climbers. There will be a primitive camp area one day, but for now we will follow a four-wheeler trail to the base of the mountain and then bushwhack around either side of it—there is no way to get lost since you will always come back to the same spot! Part way around the east (right) side there is a narrow passageway to the top (UTM 508217E, 3970926N), and if you go up, be sure to hike to the far end, to the official "Stack Rock" area for a terrific view of the bluffline and of the country that is spread out in front of you (UTM 508220E, 3971218N). There is a terrific view of both sunrise and sunset from the point, but if you spend the night up there be sure you don't sleepwalk! When I was much younger we hunted around and found the grave of someone who once lived up on top of this mountain—I'm sure the grave is still there.

To reach the parking area (now just a wide spot in the road at UTM 507750E, 3969713N, but eventually will be an official trailhead or road into the primitive campsite), follow the directions to Dry Creek (previous pages) and then continue on the forest road for .8 mile and park on the road. Look for a four-wheeler trail on the left, across the road, and follow it .6 mile over to the base of the bluffs (UTM 507843E, 3970544N). Then simply follow along the base to either the left or right and make the entire circle or return any time you like (it is 1.2 miles around the base of the mountain). There are also many giant chunks of sandstone that have rolled off of the bluff that make for interesting exploration.

Stack Rock

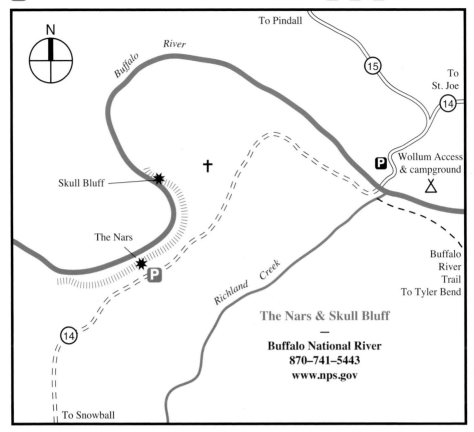

THE NARS and SKULL BLUFF. A photo of Skull Bluff is one thing that first drew me to the Buffalo River area more than 30 years ago (UTM 508980E, 3980466N). I don't know of anyplace else quite like it. The tall limestone bluff comes right down into a large deep hole of water in the river and over eons several pockets have been weathered out of the bluff, leaving the "skull" openings that you can actually drive a canoe right into. I like to camp on the gravel bar opposite this bluff so that I can enjoy the still waters in the evening and again at first light the next morning. It is an absolutely wonderful swimming hole even in the driest of summers.

Just upstream from Skull Bluff, the "Nars" or Narrows is where a ridge of stone has been eroded into a narrow fin of exposed rock by both the Buffalo River and Richland Creek that have flowed within a few feet of each other over time. Richland Creek has receded to the other side of its wide valley but the Buffalo River still flows at the base of this rock formation. You can scramble to the top from the Buffalo River, but you can also reach the top from a county road that is at the base on the other side, although getting to that road when water levels are high is often impossible without a long hike. The view from up there is pretty nice, especially when you look back down at the fin of rock that is only a couple of feet wide in some places. It is extremely dangerous up there so be sure and watch your step! (UTM 508811E, 3979969N)

Both rock formations are located upstream from Woolum (1.5 to 2 miles), so any float that takes you to Woolum will bring you past them (Mt. Hersey is the closest put-in, 6.5 miles upstream). It is also possible to paddle upstream from Woolum if you dare. When the river is low you can drive across the Buffalo River at Woolum (high-clearance

The Nars (above); Skull Bluff (below)

4wd vehicles only), go 1.2 miles on CR#14 and park—the road is very narrow. You can scramble up to the top of The Nars on either end (look for the unmarked scramble paths). If brave enough you may be able to climb down the other side of the bluff to the river and hike/swim downstream .5 mile to Skull Bluff. You can also reach the Nars by taking CR#12/Richland Rd. from Snowball for 5.0 miles, then TURN RIGHT onto CR#14/N. Richland Road and go 3.6 miles park (this road fords Richland Creek so you can only take it when the water is low). Finally, the Ozark Highlands Trail goes right past the Nars at mile 163.7 (12.1 miles from the Stack Rock Trailhead).

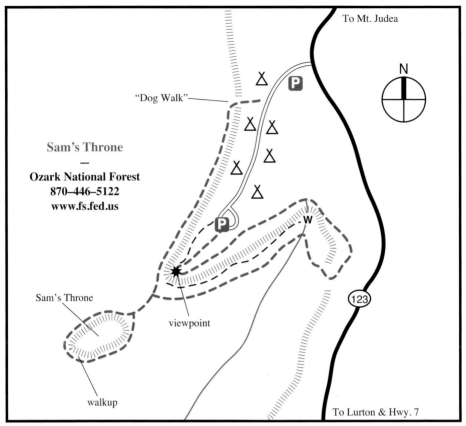

SAM'S THRONE has long been a mecca for rock climbers from around the country, but they now have improved the access and camping facilities there and it is a great scenic spot and hiking area. If you just want to have a quick look at the "throne" you can hike a short trail down to a great vista, or you can hike the loop trail and visit both the top and bottom of these spectacular bluffs and go hike around the base of Sam's Throne (and walk up on top of it if you like). The throne was named after a guy who used to preach from the top, but the bluffs are its real fame, and you will love them.

To get to the easy viewpoint, simply drive all the way to the end of the road and park at the circle drive, then hike the short trail down the hill a couple hundred yards to the top of the bluff. NOTE: all of this area can get crowded on popular climbing weekends! Climbers are good folks, and sure do know their scenery. OK, now for the longer hike, park back at the main parking area near the main entrance. About 100 yards after you pass through the gates TURN RIGHT onto an unofficial trail that drops down the hill and goes down through a split in the bluffline called the "Dog Walk" (UTM 495743E, 3970185N)—TURN LEFT and follow the trail along the bottom of the bluffs. This is a trail that has been beat down by years of use so is easy to follow but not marked. These bluffs are really quite amazing, and it is no wonder climbers have been attracted to them for so long. The trail will eventually come out to just below the main viewpoint and veer to the RIGHT and head on through a level saddle and then up to the base of the Sam's Throne bluffs—go either right or left to encircle the throne and you will end up back at this same point. There is a spot near the far southwest end of the bluff where you can scramble up through a crack in the bluff to the top—quite an impressive view (UTM 495261E,

View of Sam's Throne from the main viewpoint (above); under the bluff (below)

3969379N). It is 1.0 miles from the parking area to that point.

Return to the saddle and head back towards the main bluff and take a trail to the RIGHT that is actually an old roadbed. This will take you below the southern bluffs, but down in the woods a little ways (you can hike along the very base of the bluffs as well), and eventually the old road will switchback up towards the highway through a break in the bluffline—TURN LEFT here off of the old road (UTM 496134E, 3969717N). This trail will take you back along the top of the big bluffs to the main viewpoint, then TURN RIGHT and head up the hill to the campground and back to the parking area (there are actually two trails from the viewpoint to the campground and either one is fine) for a total loop of 2.75 miles.

To get to Sam's Throne, take Hwy. 123 from Lurton (between Jasper and Dover on Hwy. 7) and go 10 miles and TURN LEFT at the Sam's Throne sign. There is a parking area on the left, or continue straight ahead through the gate to the primitive camp area where the road ends in a circle drive.

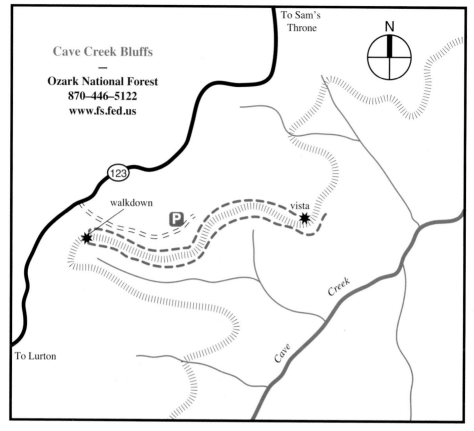

CAVE CREEK BLUFFS is another great rock climbing area that is not used as much as Sam's Throne, however there are some really nice views from on top and terrific rock and bluff formations below. Since this area does not get much use, there are really no beat-down trails, and you will be bushwhacking most of the way as you please. What I like to do is head straight down to the top edge of the bluff from the parking area and walk to the right, along the bluffline until I get to the main "walkdown" location (UTM 494823E, 3966302N). This is a pretty neat spot but you have to climb down through a crevice in between the bluff and a giant rock to get down below the bluff. From there you can follow along the base of the bluff over to the right, but the main part of the bluffline is back to the LEFT. Probably your best bet is to look around awhile and then return via the same route. If you are really into exploring, continue on around the base of the bluff. There are several locations where you are able to climb up through the bluff, but these are unmarked and are difficult climbs (UTM 495426E, 3966178N; UTM 495635E, 3966409N plus others). The best scenic views from the top of the bluff are on the far end (UTM 496108E, 3966415N), and also to the south of the main walkdown location noted above (for a winter sunrise perhaps?).

To reach this less-popular scenic area, start from the turnoff into Sam's Throne and head back towards Lurton on Hwy. 123. Go 3.2 miles and TURN LEFT onto a 4wd road—there will be a mudhole right at the beginning (UTM 494745E, 3966510N). You can either park here and hike down the road or drive in another .25 mile and park if you have a high-clearance vehicle (rough road). The bluffs will be on your right just a couple hundred feet into the woods.

*One of the scenic vistas from on top of the bluff (above);
and looking up from below (below)*

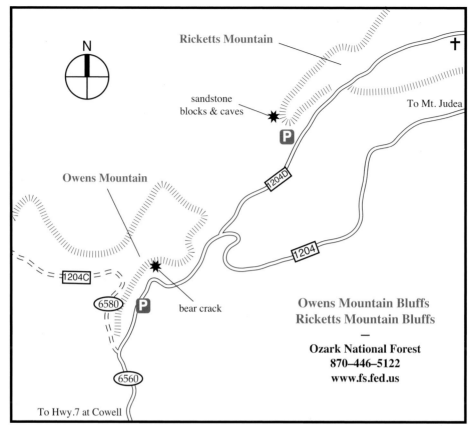

OWENS MOUNTAIN BLUFFS is another great scenic bluff area that is easy to get to right off of the road. It kind of reminds me of a giant frozen wave of sandstone, and it arches high overhead as you walk its base. There is a giant block that has broken away from the bluff near the south end that is interesting, and at the far end of the main bluffline there is a "crack" that you can climb up through, all the way to the top (UTM 488450E, 3969697N). The bluff continues on, curving around to the north where you will find more and more great stuff. NOTE: there are pictographs on the bluffs here and everything is protected! You can drive near the top of the bluffs on FR#1204C if you need to.

To get to Owens Mountain go east on FR#1204/CR#6560 from Cowell (located 17 miles south of Jasper on Hwy. 7) for 5.4 miles and park at the wide spot in the road. The bluffs are across the road and up the hill about 100 yards.

RICKETTS MOUNTAIN BLUFFS is one of the most unique rock formations you will ever see, and they're only 100 feet from your car! (UTM 489056E, 3970287N) This is another rock climbing area few other people know about, and you can even take your kids to this one, although be careful if you get up on top with them. There are a series of sandstone boulders along the base of the bluff with caves and overhangs all over the place, plus you can make your way up through a split in the bluff and find "turtle rocks" up there, and also a great sweeping view of the sunset, and in the winter, of the sunrise too.

To get to Ricketts Mountain, simply continue on from the parking area above for .5 mile and TURN LEFT on FR#1204D at the sign for Ricketts Mtn. Cemetery. Go .4 mile and pull in to the LEFT and park at the base of the bluffs.

The wave of sandstone on Owens Mountain (above); one of the many tunnels at Ricketts Mountain (left). Look for the person in both photos for scale.

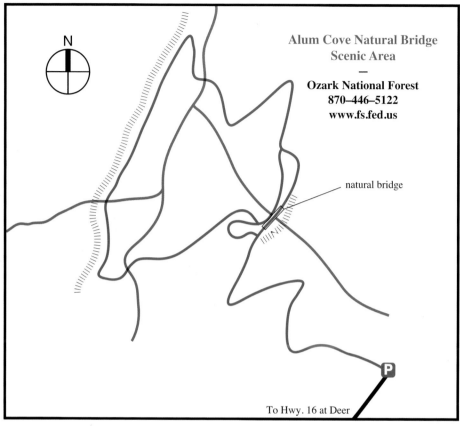

Alum Cove Natural Bridge Scenic Area
—
**Ozark National Forest
870–446–5122
www.fs.fed.us**

natural bridge

N

To Hwy. 16 at Deer

ALUM COVE NATURAL BRIDGE SCENIC AREA has one of the largest and most impressive stone arches in this part of the country. In fact, they used to drive across it. And if you are there at the right time of the year, you can catch the sun rising underneath it. But the arch is just one part of this easy loop trail, and you will find other places to explore on the opposite bluffline too, including a rare shooting star wildflower and interesting sandstone formations. The trail does drop down the hillside a bit, which means you will have to climb out, but it is a gradual grade and you won't be in a hurry, anyway, so take your time.

     To get to the picnic area/trailhead from the community of Deer, go north out of town on Hwy. 16 and TURN LEFT onto FR#1206/CR#8766 (paved), then go about three miles and TURN RIGHT at the sign and park at the picnic area. The trail begins right out in front and drops down the hill to the natural bridge, then heads to a small creek below and then up to the bluffline across the way. After following the bluffline for a little bit, the trail loops back to the natural bridge and up to the parking area.

The natural bridge from below

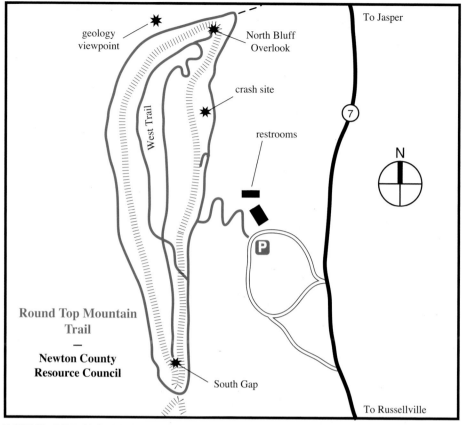

ROUND TOP MOUNTAIN TRAIL is a great scenic destination that is right off of the highway south of Jasper. It is known for a WW II-era B-25 bomber that crashed in 1948 (the trail goes right past the crash site), but I love it for the spectacular bluffline that you can follow all the way around the mountain, the great views from up on top of the bluff, and especially for the spectacular wildflower *explosion* that happens in the springtime. In fact, I know of only one other location in the area that can match the tremendous wild-flower display along this trail (at Lost Valley). There are often dozens of different species in bloom at the same time, but also I've seen literally hundreds and hundreds of one of my favorite species in bloom together creating a carpet of yellow along the trail—yellow trout lilies. The soil along the bench that the trail follows must be really rich to produce such a profusion of wildflowers. But that only happens in the springtime, the other sea-sons are great here too, because of the views, and the great bluffline that encircles the mountain. And at the half-way point around the trail you can see a narrow fin of sand-stone that is quite interesting—you can climb up onto it as well, but watch your step!

The property is owned by the non-profit Newton County Resource Council, who built and maintains the trail. They are always looking for volunteers to help out!

To reach the trailhead, go south from Jasper on Hwy. 7 a couple of miles and TURN RIGHT at the hiker sign and park at the top of the circle drive near the little building.

Check with the Jasper Chamber of Commerce at 800–670–7792 more area info.

Round Top Mountain (above); yellow trout lilies (below)

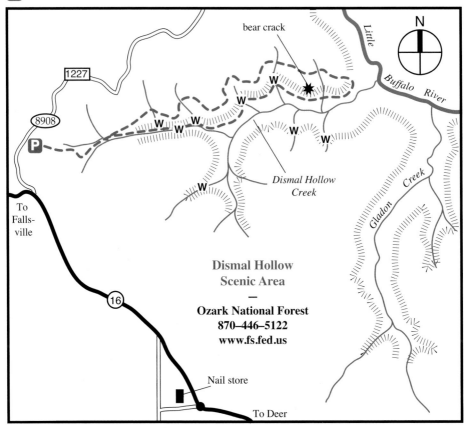

DISMAL HOLLOW SCENIC AREA. This place certainly does not live up to its name, since it is one of the most scenic areas I know of and the only "dismal" part is having to go home! There are no trails or parking areas here, and any route into the area will be difficult bushwhacking, but if you are a serious backcountry explorer, you will be rewarded with waterfalls, giant blufflines, scenic vistas, the "bear crack," and some really wonderful wilderness landscape. I keep going back again and again and still have many photos left to capture. I will describe the route that I normally take, but it covers only a small part of the area.

To get to the parking area from Nail (on Hwy. 16 west of Deer), go west on Hwy. 16 for 1.5 miles and TURN RIGHT (north) onto FR#1227/CR#8908. Go .45 mile and PARK on the right side of the road. Look around and you will find an old logging road that goes to the right (east) from the low point and heads downhill. Follow this road until it makes a big swing to the right and runs kind of level for a little bit, and then leave the road to the LEFT and drop down into the drainage below—all of the drainages will feed into the main one so just hike downhill and you will find the main creek, which has a solid rock bottom. You will eventually come to a large bluffline that begins on the left side of the stream and the scenic stuff begins! Just keep following that bluffline, and it will take you past a thundering waterfall on the main creek (photo at right, UTM 473466E, 3966780N), and into a forest of umbrella magnolias and some giant hardwoods. The bluffline will leave the creek and continue on past several large waterfalls that pour over the bluff—some have deep overhangs behind the falls. The bluff will curve around to the left (with more waterfalls) as the creek falls away far below. Just as the bluffline enters

The first waterfall along the bushwhack route (above); umbrella magnolia bloom (right)

the Little Buffalo River canyon, you can climb up on top of the bluff (great view) and begin to make your way back along the top of the bluff. There is a "bear crack" at one point (UTM 474994E, 3967183N) that leads down into the center part of the bluff, but not all the way to the bottom. Continue on along the top until you loop back to where you first encountered the bluffline, then climb back out to your car. This will be a total of 6-7 miles, although it will feel more like twenty!

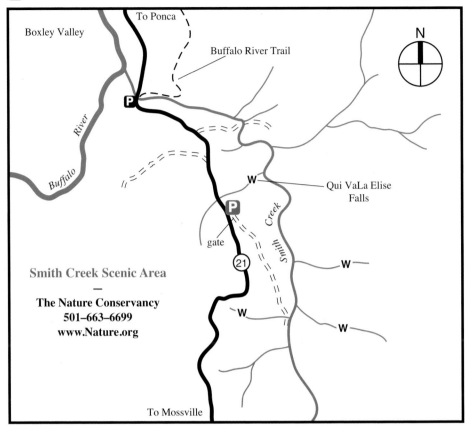

SMITH CREEK SCENIC AREA is a great 1100-acre scenic area at the south end of Boxley Valley that is protected by The Nature Conservancy and is being explored for its scenic qualities. There are more beautiful cascades that tumble over moss-covered rocks here than anyplace else I know. Towering bluffs. Waterfalls. Giant chunks of rock clogging the stream, and more wildflowers than you can count. Smith Creek runs throughout the heart of this area (and into the Buffalo River downstream) and during high water is a favorite of kayakers. But even when the creek is bone dry (which is frequent), I find great beauty in the solid mass of boulders you'll often see covering the streambed—it is possible in some areas to hop from boulder to boulder for a hundred yards! An extensive cave system runs under the property (in fact the stream often completely disappears right into it), and is home to an endangered species of bat, which is one reason The Nature Conservancy has protected the land.

There are a few old road traces that are converted to trails, and also a good road that runs from the parking area just off the highway (the road is gated so you will be hiking on it) for about a mile on down the hillside to the creek in the bottom. From there you can explore upstream (.3 mile upstream is one of the most spectacular spots—UTM 465982E, 3974781N) or downstream, and have access to the many side drainages where all of the cascades live. Far downstream in one side canyon is Qui VaLa Elise Falls that I named after Elise Roenigk, who along with her husband Martin, were responsible for the area being protected (UTM UTM 465469E, 39 76940N). There are many old, grown-up logging roads through the area that you can follow to unknown delights.

A cascade in one of the many side canyons that are worth exploring

From the south end of Boxley Valley take Hwy. 21 south up the steep hill for 1.2 miles and TURN LEFT onto the little dirt road and park near the gate at the tall sign (don't block). Or from the Mossville church head north on Hwy. 21 for 3.2 miles.

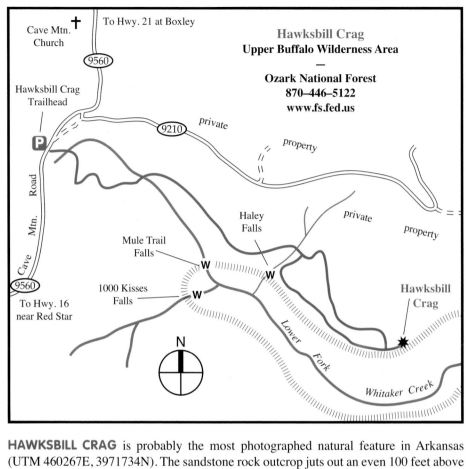

HAWKSBILL CRAG is probably the most photographed natural feature in Arkansas (UTM 460267E, 3971734N). The sandstone rock outcrop juts out an even 100 feet above the forest below, but when standing on it you hardly know it. This is a popular destination (known simply as the "Crag") and can get crowded on spring and fall weekends, so I suggest visiting at other times of the year, or during the week. The trail to the Crag is a beautiful hike, and passes by giant beech trees, stands of maples, and carpets of wildflowers. The trail also gives access to several waterfalls along the way, including Haley Falls (UTM 459685E, 3972020 N), named after the six-year old girl who got lost near this falls and was found three days later several miles away (safe). The view from the Crag out into the Upper Buffalo Wilderness Area is amazing, and you can often hear the thundering waters of Whitaker Creek far below. (NOTE: there is no official trail PAST the Crag, and it does NOT LOOP BACK to the trailhead—if you go to the Crag you must TURN AROUND and hike back from the creek that forms Haley Falls to reach the trailhead.) Most of the trail to the Crag is a one-way trail that you hike in and back out again on the same trail. However there are two routes between the Haley Falls area and the Crag itself—a high route along an old roadbed, and a low route that follows along the top of the blufline—see the map above. The blufline route is a little bit longer, but more scenic. There are several "volunteer" trails developing just above the Crag, and there are a couple of trails that head off to private property. It is easy to get confused by all of the trails so the best bet is simply to retrace your steps from the Crag back to the trailhead.

From Ponca take Hwy. 43 south through Boxley Valley to the intersection

Sunrise at the "Crag"

with Hwy. 21. TURN LEFT and go south on Hwy. 21 for 1.2 miles (over two bridges) and TURN RIGHT onto Cave Mountain Road/CR#9560 (gravel) just before the bridge over the Buffalo River (zero your odometer). The road goes *steeply* up Cave Mountain (big RVs not recommended). You will pass Cave Mountain Church at 5.4, and come to the Hawksbill Crag Trailhead at 6.0. OR from Hwy. 16 at Red Star (between Pettigrew and Fallsville) go .6 mile east on Hwy. 16 and TURN LEFT onto CR#3595 (becomes CR#9560) and go 7.0 miles to the trailhead.

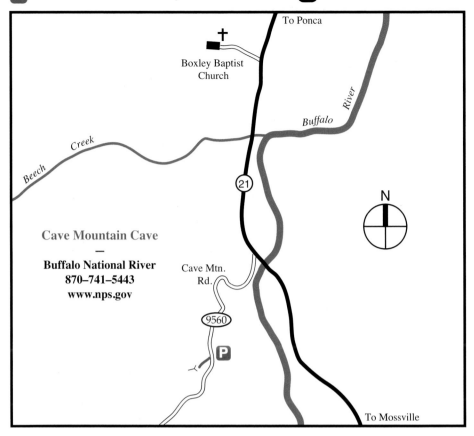

CAVE MOUNTAIN CAVE* was being used by confederate soldiers during the Civil War until Union troops raided the operation and destroyed many of the 14 buildings there. The soldiers were mining bat guano and using it in the production of saltpeter, which was used to make black powder. Seven giant iron kettles that were in use there were broken up by the invading troops, but you can see one of them right along the highway in Boxley Valley (see next listing). Bats also play a role in modern-day use of the cave as endangered Indiana and gray bats spend winters in the cave, so to keep from disturbing their colonies the cave entrance is closed off and no entry permitted between August 15th and May 15th*. But during the summer this is a great wild cave to explore! You won't find high-decorated passages like you will in the commercial caves of the area, but you will find lots of rooms and corridors to explore, many it seems are nothing but solid mud. The lawyers won't allow me to talk about any particular route inside the cave, but I will say: be sure to wear a hard hat, take three sources of light, take plenty of water and snacks and a first aid kit, and go with at least two other folks. Oh yes, and bring along a spare change of clothes for the ride home since yours will be covered with cave mud!

To reach the parking area from Ponca, take Hwy. 43 south through Boxley Valley to the intersection with Hwy. 21. TURN LEFT and go south on Hwy. 21 for 1.2 miles (over two bridges) and TURN RIGHT onto Cave Mtn. Road/CR#9560 (gravel) just before the bridge over the Buffalo River. The road goes *steeply* up Cave Mountain (too steep for big RVs and no room to park or turnaround) and the parking area will be on your LEFT after .45 mile. Walk across the road and up the trail for about a hundred yards to the cave entrance.

*NOTE: the cave may be closed due to vandalism—call the park service for latest info.

A caver standing in the entrance to the cave (above);
one of the iron kettles that was destroyed by Union troops (below)

By the way there is a great sunrise viewpoint nearby (not good in the summer though). Continue past the Cave Mountain Trailhead for 1.0 miles and park on the LEFT at a small pullout. There is a giant bluffline just below the road on your left (requires a steep scramble through the woods to get down to it), and there are several great views out over the Upper Buffalo Wilderness where you can catch the sunrise—don't get too close to the edge!

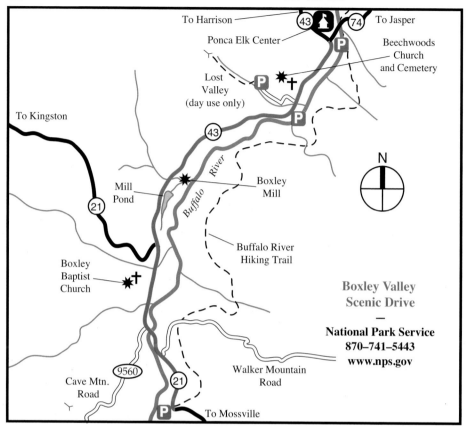

BOXLEY VALLEY SCENIC DRIVE will take you through one of the most tranquil, historical, and scenic valleys in the state. The Boxley Valley Historical District is part of Buffalo National River park and you'll pass by historical buildings and farmsteads, an old gristmill, and cemeteries with headstones dating back to the 1840's. You may also see a thriving herd of elk, and hear the big bulls bugle and fight with others in the fall. Bald eagles frequent the area, and the old Mill Pond right in the middle of it all seems to attract all sorts of wildlife, like herons, ducks, turtles, geese, and even a pair of trumpeter swans. Stop in at the Elk Center in beautiful downtown Ponca during your visit, look at all their exhibits and inquire about current elk activity.

Begin the drive at the south end of Ponca, where Hwys. 43 and 74 meet, and proceed south through the valley. There is a historical barn right at the beginning, and a farmstead from the 1800's just across the low water bridge (Ponca Access) that you can explore. On the main road, the fields on the left are where the elk herds often hang out, and the best time to view them is before and just after sunrise and just before dark. Take the turnoff to Lost Valley at 1.0 mile and then make a quick right turn and you'll find the old Beechwoods Cemetery, or continue on into Lost Valley (see next page). Continue on the main road 2.8 miles and you'll see one of the old iron kettles that was damaged by Union troops up at Cave Mountain Cave sitting in the field next to a neat old barn. NOTE: most of this property is private so be sure to look from the highway! After you pass other historical buildings you will come to a small house on the left at 3.4 miles that is covered with stone veneer, and a lane that goes past it to the Boxley Mill that was built in 1870. Just beyond this turnoff is the Mill Pond that stretches along the highway for several hundred yards and is often where you can find all sorts of wildlife, so drive s-l-o-w.

Mill Pond at sunrise (top); bull elk in summer velvet (above)

When you get to the intersection at 4.3 miles TURN LEFT onto Hwy. 21 and drive past a steam-powered sawmill on the left at 4.6 miles (big smoke stack), Boxley Church at 4.8 miles, past the turnoff to Cave Mountain Road/CR#9560 at 5.6 miles, then cross the Buffalo River, and finally to the south end of the valley at 6.8 miles where the Buffalo River Trail begins. At the back end of this short drive is Whiteley Spring which provides water for many folks up on Cave Mountain to this day (including me when our well goes dry). You are likely to see elk grazing out in the fields early and late in the day at any time of the year. And the quality of light early and late from one end of this valley to the other is very nice.

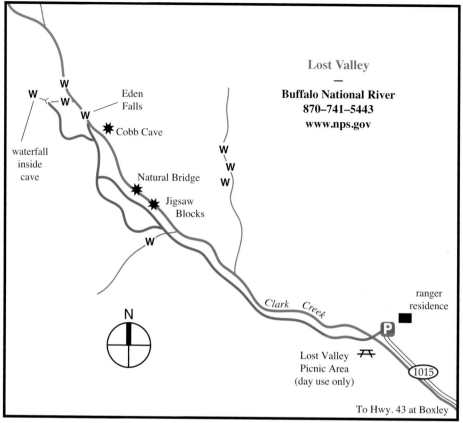

Lost Valley
—
Buffalo National River
870–741–5443
www.nps.gov

LOST VALLEY is perhaps the most scenic of all short and easy Arkansas trails, and some of it is even wheelchair-accessible. There are three main attractions to me along this trail. First and foremost, would be Eden Falls at the far end—one of the more scenic waterfalls in the land. And then you have the giant overhang right next to it called Cob Cave (named after some ancient corn cobs found there many years ago). Climb up to the very back and look out and you will get a sense of how huge this overhang is. And then climb to the very end of the trail that ends at Eden Falls Cave—the creek comes flowing right out of it, and if you remembered to bring your flashlight you will be able to explore this wild cave! The passage does not go back too far and it is impossible to get lost, although you may have to duck down really low in a spot or two. The passageway ends in a room that has a 30-foot tall waterfall in it—one of the more unique waterfalls I've seen. You can stand up and walk around but good luck getting a good photo of this waterfall.

Actually I meant there are FOUR main attractions to this place—in the early spring the landscape along the trail comes alive with carpets of wildflowers as far as you can see—one of the greatest wildflower displays in all of Arkansas! One of the main species is Ozark wake robin that is only found in a few places, yet there are hundreds of them here.

To reach Lost Valley from Ponca take Hwy. 43 into Boxley Valley for a mile and TURN RIGHT at the sign onto CR#1015 (paved, then gravel), then park at the end of the road and picnic area (the turnoff is 3.3 miles from the Hwys. 43 & 21 intersection, then turn left into the park). The trail is wide and well used and sometimes crowded and will be easy to follow.

Eden Falls from inside Cobb Cave (above); yellow trout lily and liverleaf (below)

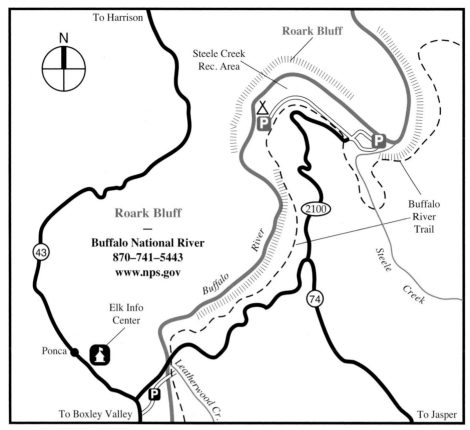

ROARK BLUFF is the longest and most painted of all the limestone bluffs along the Buffalo River. Water stains from different minerals provide lots of color to the bluff. While you can see the bluff from your car, it is a level and easy walk to get right on over to the base of the bluff, where you can get the full effect of the long sweeping bluffline that reaches skyward for 220 feet. Park your car near either end of the bluffline, or somewhere in the middle and hike on over. This is one place I can always count on at any time of the year to produce a great scene for me to photograph. One of my favorite images came in the dead of winter when I waded out into the rapids at the downstream end of a long still pool. I wanted to capture the reflection of the bluff but also how the ripples distorted the reflection. I spent so much time out in that nearly-frozen water that when it was time for me to wade back to shore I had lost all feeling in my legs and I nearly fell into the river!

To get to Roark Bluff, which is located at the Steele Creek Recreation Area, simply take Hwy. 74 from Ponca, across the big bridge over the river towards Jasper and TURN LEFT onto CR#2100 (paved) at the big entrance way after all the curves (at the top of the hill), then proceed down the road (several sharp switchbacks) to the bottom of the hill (road becomes gravel)—Roark Bluff will be spread out in front of you to the left (turn left to drive back to the campground).

Roark Bluff reflected in the Buffalo River

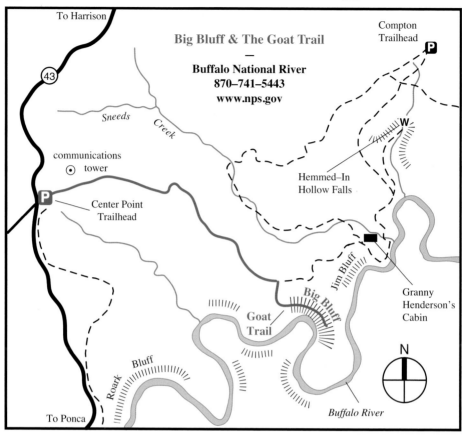

BIG BLUFF and The GOAT TRAIL. There are many tall bluffs along the Buffalo River, but Big Bluff has long been considered the tallest of them all at more than 500 feet. It is located in the middle of the Ponca Wilderness Area, and just off one of the main access trails into Hemmed-In Hollow. The side trail that goes down to and across Big Bluff is called the Goat Trail. (Not to be confused with the Goat Bluff Trail in the Erbie area downstream.) This is not a place for young kids, drunks, or those who are afraid of heights. When you are out on the Goat Trail there is 320 feet of air out over the edge between you and the Buffalo River (a number of folks have fallen to their deaths here). It is one of the more stunning views in the wilderness, and a place hikers continue to flock to.

To reach Big Bluff, take Hwy. 43 north out of Ponca and TURN RIGHT into the Center Point Trailhead after 3.5 miles. Hike down the trail (along an old road) for 2.7 miles and TURN RIGHT onto the small trail, which will come out onto Big Bluff in .25 mile. While it is possible to keep going at the end of the bluff trail, it is best to enjoy the view and then return to the main trail. If you continued along the main trail, it would take you down to the Buffalo River, past Granny Henderson's cabin, and over to Hemmed-In Hollow (the long way in). The return trip back to the trailhead can get a little steep, so plan plenty of time.

Looking down on the Buffalo River from The Goat Trail on Big Bluff (note hiker)

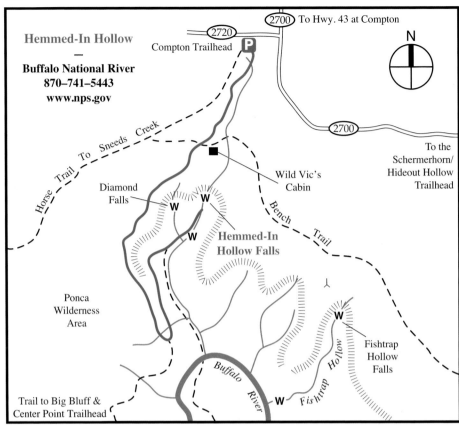

Hemmed-In Hollow
—
Buffalo National River
870–741–5443
www.nps.gov

HEMMED-IN HOLLOW is the tallest free-falling waterfall between the Rocky Mountains and the Appalachians at 209 feet, and during high water it is one spectacular sight to see. Even when there is little or no water, the painted bluffs that guard the hollow are quite scenic. And when the wind is blowing, the ribbon of water is so tall that the water is whipped around like a horsetail—quite a refreshing splash if you happen to be standing at the bottom! It is possible to scramble up the steep hillside and get behind the falls, and even follow the bluffline around to the left to another tall falls that Neil Compton named Diamond Falls. This is steep, rugged country, and some of the best you will ever visit.

The short way into the falls is from the Compton Trailhead. It is only 2.5 miles down to the falls but it will feel like 20 miles on the way—the trail is steep, rugged, and more than a thousand foot climb back up so be sure to plan an entire day for the trip.

The turnoff for the trailhead is located at Compton, between Harrison and Ponca on Hwy. 43. Take the gravel road across from the post office in Compton (CR#2700), TURN RIGHT at the first intersection, and go just less than a mile and TURN RIGHT onto CR#2720 and then LEFT into the trailhead parking lot. There are two trails that leave this lot—the one on the right is a horse trail that goes down to Sneeds Creek and beyond. For a longer hike you can return on this trail and make a 7.2 mile loop.

When the water is high and really cooking there is a "twin" falls just downstream from the main waterfall that is worth a look. Winter is a great time to visit waterfalls in the Ozarks—that is when you will often find the waterfalls flowing full tilt, and the Buffalo River area has many great ones.

Hemmed-In Hollow Falls as seen from the trail on the way in (above);
twin falls downstream of the main waterfall (below)

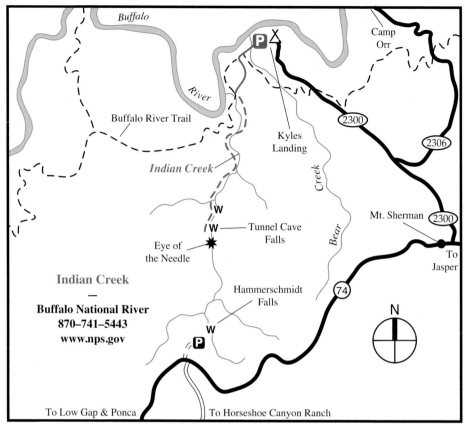

INDIAN CREEK contains waterfalls, towering bluffs, fern-covered hillsides, the "Eye of the Needle," and is some of the most rugged and dangerous terrain in the Ozarks. There is no official trail through the area, and the park service reports more injuries from here than anyplace else—proceed into this area with caution and only if you are willing to face dangerous and difficult terrain. If you go and make it out alive, the sights are spectacular!

It is possible to come in from the top of the drainage past Hammerschmidt Falls—take Hwy. 74 east from Low Gap 2.4 miles (or 2.8 miles west from the turnoff to Kyles Landing) and turn north onto a jeep road (directly across from the turnoff into Horseshoe Canyon Ranch) and park at the end of the road. It is a TOUGH climb all the way down the canyon. I prefer to come in from the bottom and work my way up to such great sights like Arkansas Cave and the Eye of the Needle, and then return back out the same way. To get to the bottom from Jasper, go west on Hwy. 74 to Mt. Sherman and TURN RIGHT at the sign for Kyles Landing on CR#2300 (OR go east from Low Gap on Hwy. 74 for 5.2 miles to Mt. Sherman and TURN LEFT at the Kyles Landing Sign). Go 1.0 mile and TURN LEFT at the fork, then go 1.6 miles down a steep hill to the Kyles Landing Campground. TURN LEFT after the bathhouse and go all the way back to the trailhead and PARK.

From the trailhead hike upstream on the Buffalo River Trail and just before you get to Indian Creek TURN LEFT and follow the unofficial trail up into the canyon. It will cross the creek a few times, and climb high on the hillsides, but eventually it will lead you right to a dead-end—this is where the really scenic stuff begins! There is a waterfall that comes right out of the mouth of Arkansas Cave (or Tunnel Cave) and drops into the creek

Tunnel Cave Falls and ferns along Indian Creek

below. This cave is closed to all entry to protect endangered bats. From that point you have to climb up a small bluff (via rope if one is present) and then carefully climb up and around and through an opening in the hillside to continue upstream. Not too far upstream you will come to the "Eye Of The Needle" that sometimes has a torrent of water pouring down it when there is a flood going on. I normally turn back at this point but it is possible to keep going up and up and up, eventually climbing up to the top of the drainage beyond Hammerschmidt Falls and coming out on Hwy. 74.

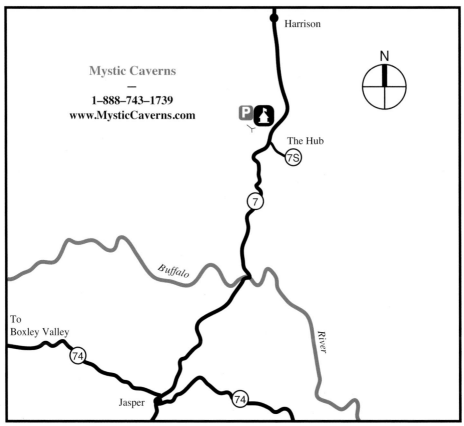

Mystic Caverns
—
1–888–743–1739
www.MysticCaverns.com

Harrison

The Hub

7S

7

Buffalo

To
Boxley Valley

74

River

Jasper

74

N

MYSTIC CAVERNS is a beautiful, highly-decorated commercial cave that is a great cave for first-time cavers to visit. In fact there are two caverns you can tour and view a variety of multicolored flowstone, columns, stalactites and stalagmites, as well as cave bacon and the rare and awesome helictite formations. All of this is located right off of Hwy. 7 in between Harrison and Jasper. It is a family-owned business and the guides have been going underground here for many years and are happy to answer just about any question you can throw at them. NOTE: the caverns are not open on Sunday.

The "Pipe Organ" formation

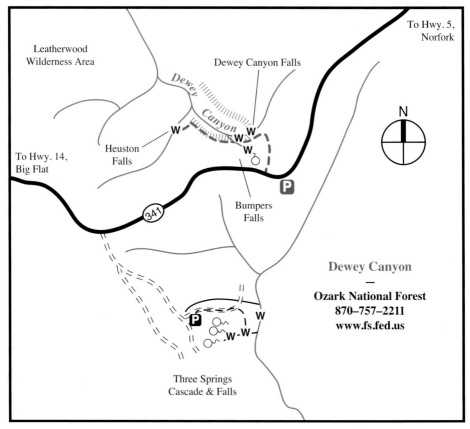

DEWEY CANYON is at the lowest end of the Buffalo River drainage, at the edge of the Leatherwood Wilderness Area. It is located only a couple hundred yards off of a main paved highway, and is a very small area, yet it is one of the most spectacular canyons in the Ozarks, especially when the water is high and the four waterfalls there are running at full tilt. I could hardly believe this place was so close to the highway the first time I visited. Be careful here since the bluff is very high and a fall would be fatal.

From Big Flat, go 3.8 miles east on Hwy. 14 and TURN LEFT onto Hwy. 341 (paved). Go 8.9 miles and PARK on the right at the beginning of the big curve.

CROSS the road and go back to the left to the beginning of a guard rail. You will find a faint trail there that heads down into the drainage to a little creek. TURN LEFT and follow the creek just a short distance to the top of 88' tall Dewey Canyon Falls (UTM 558767E, 3993984N), one of four waterfalls in this little canyon.

There are many other great waterfalls in the Leatherwood Wilderness Area—see them in the *Arkansas Waterfalls Guidebook* (also listed in waterfalls guidebook are the Three Springs Cascade & Falls that are shown on the map above, which is across the highway from the wilderness area and worth a visit if the water is running high).

Bumpers Falls (in front) and Dewey Canyon Falls (in back)

East Region

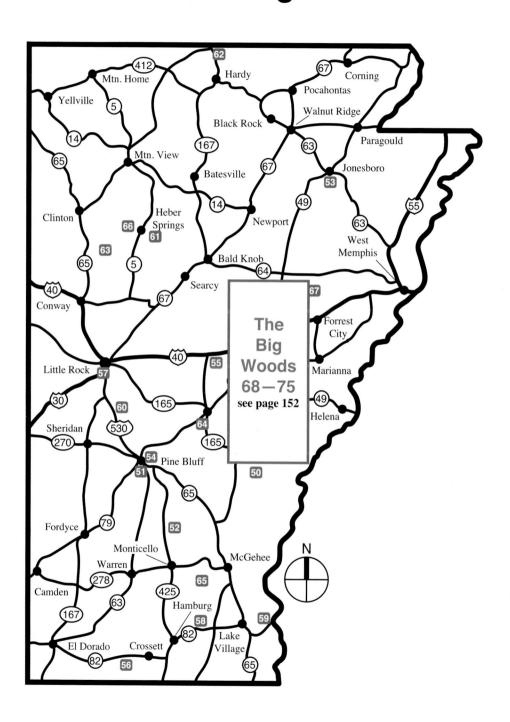

The
Big
Woods
68—75
see page 152

The EAST REGION of Arkansas is delta country, with swamps, prairies, oxbow lakes, and vast wildlife management areas where ducks and geese by the millions spend the winter. Most of the landscape is flat and seems like there is nothing for miles and miles in all directions, however there is some dramatic beauty to be found if you know where to look (in fact, some of my most favorite scenic spots in the state!). I've included a unique elephant sanctuary here, and a lake where a flock of trumpeter swans have been coming to spend the winter ever since they got blown off course by a hurricane many years ago. And we have the largest spring in the state in this region, which is also the 10th largest one in the entire world! All of the places in this region are simple to get to, with easy, level hiking trails—and in some cases, you will need a boat (oops, the Sugar Loaf Mountain trail is steep, but all the rest are level!). There are also a pair of wonderful nature centers where you can learn about the environment both inside and out. With so much interest generated lately about "The Big Woods" country of eastern Arkansas, I have created a separate section for those amazing swamp areas, which you can find on page 152.

Scenic Areas in the East Region

50

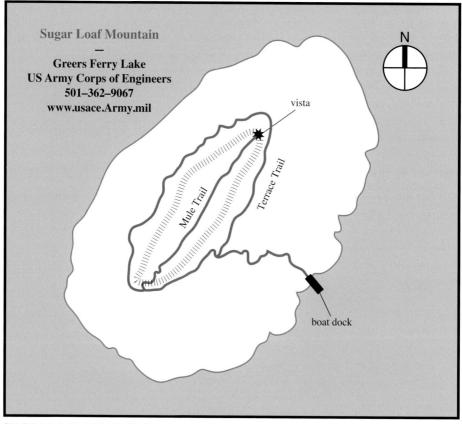

Sugar Loaf Mountain
—
Greers Ferry Lake
US Army Corps of Engineers
501–362–9067
www.usace.Army.mil

vista

Mule Trail

Terrace Trail

boat dock

N

SUGAR LOAF MOUNTAIN is an island in Greers Ferry Lake and has one of the most unique and scenic of all our hiking trails on it. Unless you are a really good swimmer, you will need a boat to get over to the island to begin the hike—it's about a half mile across the bay from the nearest boat launch ramp. This mountain island reminds me of a volcano rising up out of the sea. The trail up to the top is very scenic, and the views once you get up there are just wonderful. At one time the trail looped around the back side and climbed up to the top of the mountain, returning down the front side of the mountain to complete the loop. Now it is a one-way trail up to the top that takes you up many steps through the bluffline, but you can also hike the loop trail around the base of the bluffs if you have the time. The top part of the trail is called the Mule Trail, and the loop that goes all the way around the base is called the Terrace Trail. No camping or fires are allowed on the island.

From the dock, simply head up the wide trail as it climbs steeply up towards the base of the bluff. TURN LEFT when you get to a trail intersection (or turn right to make the loop around the base of the bluffs on the Terrace Trail—add a mile to the total distance if you do). And then TURN RIGHT and climb up through the bluffline at the next trail intersection—a great view all around for sure. Follow the Mule Trail along the spine of the mountain to the far end of the ridge where the trail ends on top of the bluff—more incredible views. To get back to the dock turn around and hike the trail back down the same way that you came up, or you could go back part way and take the loop trail around the base of the bluffs. Either way you will most likely be ready for a dip in the clear waters below when you get finished!

The view over the lake from the end of the Mule Trail

The best place to access this trail is via the Sugar Loaf Recreation Area on Greers Ferry Lake. From Heber Springs, take Hwy. 25 south for 8 miles, then go west on Hwy. 16 for 11.9 miles to Hwys. 92 & 337. Then go 2.7 miles to the park. Sugar Loaf Mountain is located northeast of the park—it's pretty easy to spot, and is a short boat ride away. The dock trailhead is located on the southeast side of the island as shown on the map.

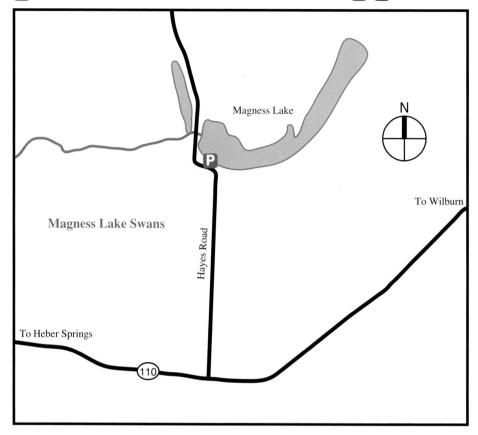

Magness Lake

N

To Wilburn

Magness Lake Swans

Hayes Road

To Heber Springs

110

MAGNESS LAKE SWANS. Many years ago a hurricane blew a flock of trumpeter swans off course and they landed on a small private lake just outside of Heber Springs. Those very same birds have been returning to Magness Lake every winter since, along with new generations of swans. This is an incredible opportunity to view these giant majestic birds up close and personal, and if you have never seen trumpeter swans, I highly recommend you make a trip to Magness Lake! The best time to view them is in the afternoon and evening—they are often out during the day feeding at other lakes, although there are almost always swans on Magness Lake. They are normally on the lake from December through February. Please don't feed the swans anything except shelled corn.

To get to the lake, drive east on Hwy. 110 from its intersection with Hwy. 5 and Hwy. 25, just east of Heber Springs. Go 3.9 miles to Sovereign Grace Baptist Church (look for the sign). Then TURN LEFT onto paved Hayes Road and you will come to the parking area for Magness Lake about a half mile down the road. This is a private lake but visitors are allowed as long as you behave yourself!

Trumpeter swans at Magness Lake

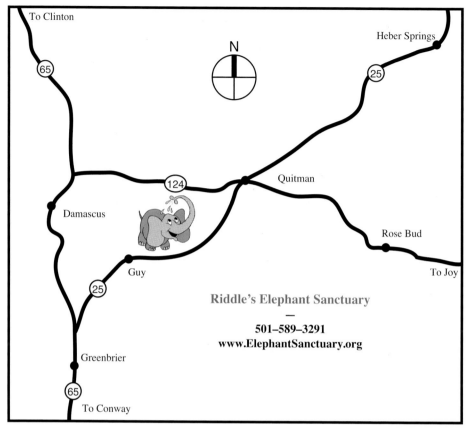

To Clinton

Heber Springs

65

25

N

124   Quitman

Damascus

Rose Bud

Guy   To Joy

25

Riddle's Elephant Sanctuary
—
501–589–3291
www.ElephantSanctuary.org

Greenbrier

65

To Conway

RIDDLE'S ELEPHANT SANCTUARY. What, elephants in Arkansas? You bet! I wanted to include this special sanctuary in this guidebook to give folks the opportunity to visit and learn about the great things the folks at the preserve are doing for these incredible creatures. They have both Asian and African elephants, and there has been some hanky-panky going on lately since they now have baby elephants that have been born at the sanctuary (and featured on Animal Planet). The elephants have been abandoned or abused and rescued by the sanctuary. The sanctuary is open to the public on the first Saturday of every month between 11am and 3pm (there is a small entrance fee), and you can view the elephants through the big fence as they go about their daily routines. If you want a really incredible experience, how about doing the "Elephant Experience Weekend!" You stay at the sanctuary and get to feed, water, groom, and even BATHE the elephants, and take them out for walks. There is no other weekend like this anywhere in the country. Learn all about the individual elephants and the sanctuary mission on their web site, and how you can adopt an elephant and help these beautiful endangered animals.

The sanctuary is located off of Hwy. 25 between Guy and Quitman—take Hwy. 65 north out of Conway and continue a couple miles past Greenbrier, then TURN RIGHT onto Hwy. 25 and proceed to the community of Guy. Go 1.0 mile past the school and TURN LEFT at the elephant sign and proceed 2.4 miles (following the signs) to the sanctuary.

*Maximus, who was born at the Sanctuary, and his mom greet visitors
(note mom's pretty eyelashes!)*

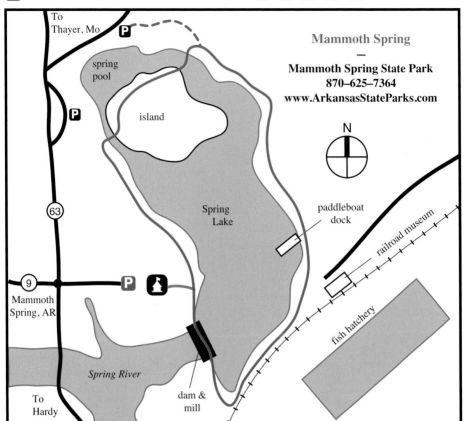

Mammoth Spring

—

Mammoth Spring State Park
870–625–7364
www.ArkansasStateParks.com

MAMMOTH SPRING is the largest spring in Arkansas and tenth largest spring in the world as it produces nearly ten million gallons of cold, clear water every hour. The spring itself and surrounding grounds are beautiful, and the lake that the spring forms is teaming with all sorts of ducks and geese that don't mind posing for photos. An easy trail (paved part of the way) goes around the small lake and it only takes a few minutes to make the loop (pick up an interpretive guide at the welcome center). This grand old spring forms the Spring River, and you can walk across the top of a dam that once provided power for a wheat mill and produced hydroelectric power. You can rent kayaks and paddle boats for a tour around the little lake, just be sure not to fall in since the water temp is below 60 degrees year-round! There is an Arkansas Welcome Center on site that has a brochure for just about every single location in The Natural State.

Once you get finished with the beautiful spring and lake area, step next door and visit the national fish hatchery and see what they are up to. They have a great aquarium and give tours and have events during the year, and stock many of the fish that are caught by sportsmen downstream. There is also a railroad museum in an old train depot built in 1886.

The park is located in Mammoth Spring at the intersection of Hwys. 63 and 9, 2 miles south of Thayer, Missouri, and 16 miles north of Hardy, Arkansas.

Mammoth Spring (above); goslings enjoying the cool water (below)

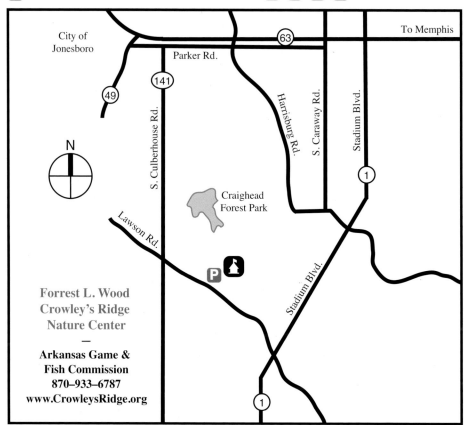

Forrest L. Wood CROWLEY'S RIDGE NATURE CENTER has a lot of neat stuff both inside and out, and is the second one of the four Game and Fish Commission nature centers to be constructed. There are several hiking trails that visit this property that was once a gravel pit (great to see how we can reclaim ugly land). One of the trails goes up to the tall Prairie Overlook structure, which is a good place to watch the sunset. There is a prairie filled with wildflowers below, and other trails that wander through the nearby forest and connect with the nearby Craighead Forest Park. There are tons of wildflower gardens scattered around the center that make great places to take flower pictures or chase butterflies during the summertime.

    Inside the center you will find all sorts of fun and interesting things to see and do—be sure to see the short film about Crowley's Ridge in the AV room—it is quite an experience! It seems like they have some sort of program going on all the time at the center for all ages, including special "howl at the moon" hikes specifically for dogs and their owners. Our tax dollars are being well spent at this facility.

    The center is located in Jonesboro between Hwy. 1 and S. Culberhouse Road. Take Hwy. 1 south from US 63 (future I-555), TURN RIGHT onto Lawson Road, and then turn into the entrance about 1.5 miles ahead on the right. NOTE: the center is not open on Mondays or most holidays, but you can park at the gate and hike the trails anytime.

Native wildflower garden and the visitor center

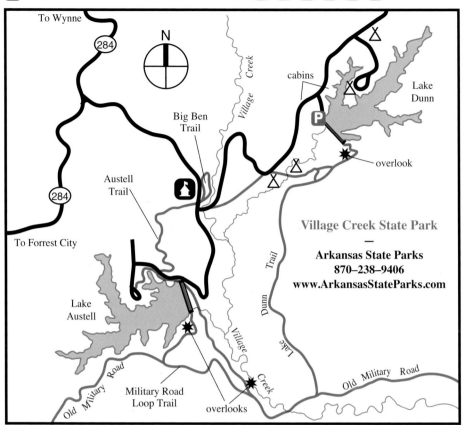

VILLAGE CREEK STATE PARK is a sprawling park (2nd largest in the system with nearly 7,000 acres) with lakes, hiking and horse trails, campgrounds, cabins, and lush beech-maple forests atop the unique geological soils of Crowley's Ridge. It is home to one of my favorite trees too—tulip poplars. The tree is actually named after the tulip-shaped leaves, but I love the large and brightly-colored blossoms that decorate the trees in springtime. The hiking trails are easy, and the lakes are full of fish. You can swim or ride horseback too, and also find a wide variety of bird and animal life throughout the park (seems to be deer everywhere, including lots of spotted fawns in the early summer).

A brand new resort is being built at Village Creek that will feature a 27-hole golf course, plus tons of meeting, lodging, and eating facilities. All of the great natural features will remain, so you will be able to make your trip a plush one, or get back to nature!

To reach the park, take exit #242 off of I-40 at Forrest City and go 13 miles north on Hwy. 284, or take Hwy. 284 south from Wynne for 6 miles.

Tulip poplar blooms (above); newborn fawn (below)

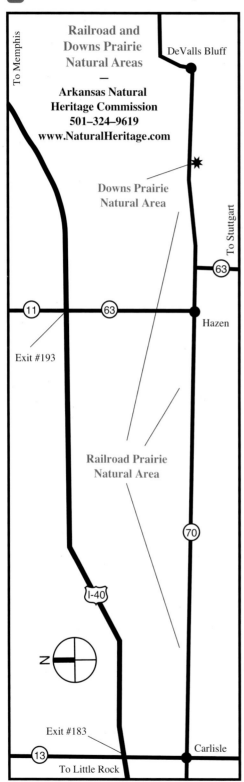

Railroad and Downs Prairie Natural Areas
—
**Arkansas Natural Heritage Commission
501–324–9619
www.NaturalHeritage.com**

DeValls Bluff

To Memphis

Downs Prairie Natural Area

To Stuttgart

63

11   63

Exit #193

Hazen

Railroad Prairie Natural Area

70

I-40

N

Exit #183

Carlisle

13

To Little Rock

RAILROAD AND DOWNS PRAIRIE NATURAL AREAS are remnants of the tallgrass prairie that once covered much of eastern Arkansas (about 320,000 acres worth). While they are actually two different tracts, I've combined them here since you can see both of them at the same time. The 250-acre Railroad Prairie is unique in that it is an old railroad right-of-way that runs for more than ten miles and was never disturbed or under cultivation all the years that the railroad was in use. You can find grasses such as big bluestem, little bluestem, and Indiangrass, along with forbs and wildflowers, like narrow-leafed sunflower, wild indigo, butterflyweed, blazing star, and many others. The smaller 30-acre tract at the eastern end of the area adds other wildflowers, including Indian paintbrush, and it is home to the rare prairie mole crickets. While you can see this entire area while zipping past in your car at 55mph, you really need to pick a spot or two and get out and walk around to see the beauty of the native wildflowers and grasses. It is a great escape from the hectic nearby interstate, and I will often detour to see the prairies while on my way east to see what is blooming during the spring and summer. There are no official parking areas—just pull over wherever you can and have a look.

To get to Railroad Prairie, take the Carlisle exit (Hwy. 13) south to Hwy. 70, then TURN LEFT (east) and head for DeValls Bluff. The prairie begins just outside of town and continues along the left (north) side of the highway all the way to DeValls Bluff. You'll find Downs Prairie just before you get to DeValls Bluff on the right (UTM 637580E, 3849643N). Both areas are Arkansas Natural Heritage Commission "Natural Areas."—and remember, as my good friend and wildflower expert, Don Kurz, always says, you can pick your nose but don't pick the wildflowers!

Smooth phlox wildflowers at Railroad Prairie

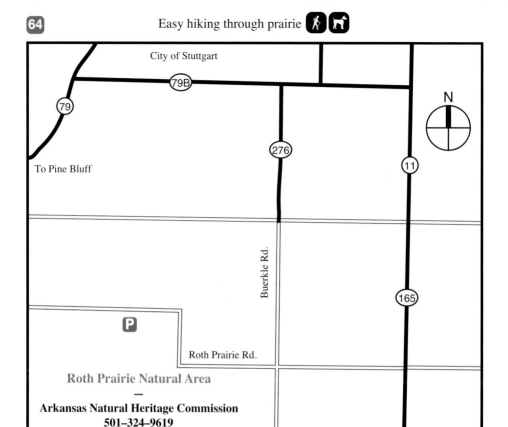

ROTH PRAIRIE NATURAL AREA is located just south of Stuttgart, in the heart of duck and rice country. It is a simple square plot of 41 acres that not only contains a wealth of native wildflowers and grasses in the spring and summer months, but also has "prairie mounds" up to three feet tall—these are an indication that the prairie had never been plowed or leveled, although it was in use as a hay field for many years before becoming a natural area. This is another great example of what was once the vast tallgrass prairie, and the local community thought enough of this area to name the road after it. One of my favorite wildflowers that seems to flourish here is the passion flower, and I've photographed it in color phases of purple, blue and even pure white. The prairie is well guarded by red-winged blackbirds, so be sure to take along a telephoto lens for your camera! Wear long pants and get out and walk this entire plot and you will find many neat wildflowers.

    To get to Roth Prairie from Stuttgart, take Hwy. 79B to Hwy. 276, then go south 1.0 mile and the road will become South Buerkle Road (gravel). Continue south on the gravel road for 1.0 mile and then TURN RIGHT onto Roth Prairie Road. You will come to the prairie after .8 mile (UTM 630726E, 3813220N), then just continue on around the perimeter until you come to the small parking area and sign at the northwest corner.

Red-wing blackbird; passion flower (inset)

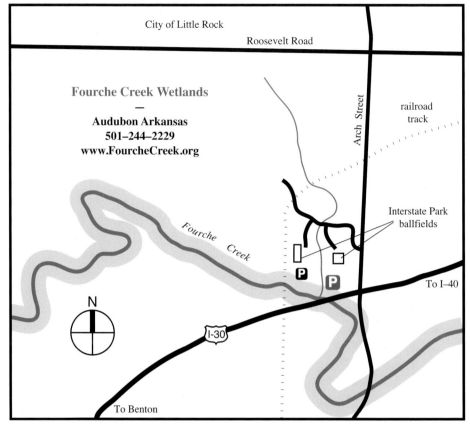

Fourche Creek Wetlands
—
Audubon Arkansas
501–244–2229
www.FourcheCreek.org

FOURCHE CREEK WETLANDS is somewhat of a surprise to folks living in Little Rock or screaming by on I-30 at 70mph—there is a beautiful cypress and tupelo swamp filled with wildlife and beautiful trees inside the city limits! This urban swamp goes for many miles and connects several city parks, although you have to hunt to find an access point, and you need a canoe or kayak to enjoy all the area has to offer. While there are some stunning ancient cypress trees along the way, the area is also somewhat of a pollution filter for storm water runoff from the city, so you will sometimes see quite a bit of trash in the water and even as part of beaver dams, not to mention the noise pollution of the nearby interstate traffic. However, once you get into the water and paddle upstream that traffic noise melts into background white noise, and you are surrounded by some really nice big trees, and you will probably forget where you are. There is a variety of wildlife—especially birds—that live in the swamp. And goodness the place really lights up with color in the fall! It is also a great place to canoe in the spring and somewhat into summer as well, although the water levels get pretty low later in the summer. Audubon Arkansas is working to preserve, protect, and clean up the swamp, and to make folks aware that a lot of city trash that ends up in the swamp could easily have been recycled in the first place—a lesson we all need to learn and practice.

     The best access point with your boat is at the Interstate Park. From I-30 take the Roosevelt Road exit (#139-A) and go west less than a mile and TURN LEFT (south) onto Arch Street, then follow it .9 mile and TURN RIGHT into the Interstate Park. There are two sets of ball fields here—the front set are baseball fields and the back set are football

Cypress trees in morning light

fields. The main boat ramp is located at the back of the baseball fields — simply follow the paved road to the left and it will end at the boat ramp (UTM 565683E, 3840780N). When water levels are low, you need to cross the ditch between the ballfields and drive across the lawn behind the scoreboard to the football field and you'll see a path that leads down to the river.

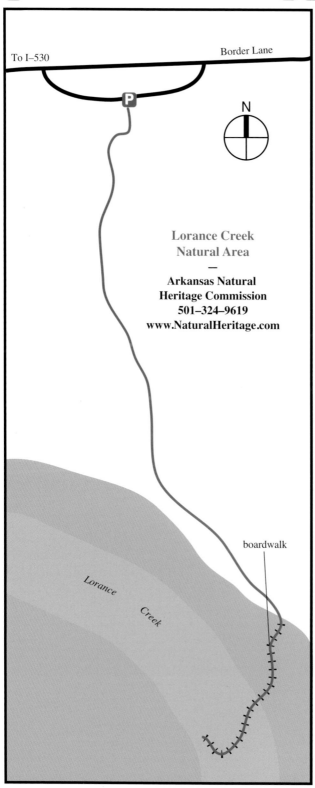

To I–530

Border Lane

P

N

Lorance Creek
Natural Area
—
**Arkansas Natural
Heritage Commission
501–324–9619
www.NaturalHeritage.com**

boardwalk

Lorance

Creek

LORANCE CREEK NATURAL AREA is a small scenic area with a paved trail and boardwalk that goes out into a dense swamp. It is located just off the interstate between Little Rock and Pine Bluff and is quick and easy to get to and to hike, and is wheelchair accessible. It's a great place to visit any time of the year, but especially in the early spring when things begin to bloom, and again in the fall when the hardwoods turn color.

From Little Rock, take I-530 south approximately 10 miles, exit at Bingham Road (Exit 9). TURN LEFT (east) on Bingham Road, cross over the interstate, and continue through a residential area. At the first "Y" in the road, go RIGHT on Bingham Road. At the second "Y" in the road, bear RIGHT on Border Lane and the Lorance Creek parking lot is a couple hundred yards on the right. Take the paved trail down into the woods and it will lead to the boardwalk into the swamp.

The boardwalk into the swamp over Lorance Creek

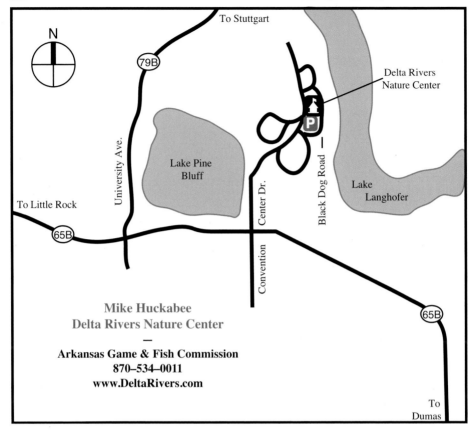

N

To Stuttgart

79B

Delta Rivers
Nature Center

P

University Ave.

Lake Pine
Bluff

Black Dog Road

Lake
Langhofer

To Little Rock

Center Dr.

65B

Convention

Mike Huckabee
Delta Rivers Nature Center

—

Arkansas Game & Fish Commission
870–534–0011
www.DeltaRivers.com

65B

To
Dumas

Mike Huckabee DELTA RIVERS NATURE CENTER, in Pine Bluff, was the first of the four big nature centers to be built by the Game and Fish Commission, and like those that followed, it is a great facility both inside and out. There are some neat water features as you approach the center where you can see fish and water plants, plus lots of wildflowers all over the place. Around back you'll find an "alligator theater" where you'll normally find a real live and large alligator splashing in the water, plus they normally have at least one captive bald eagle that you can view. That is just the beginning of the outdoor fun here—the paved Delta View hiking trail will take you into the deep woods and along the edges of small lakes and bayous where you can see all sorts of critters on the land and in the trees (new paved and primitive trails have recently been added). Sometimes I'll even make this loop twice just to make sure I didn't miss anything. If you go early or late in the day and are really quiet, you'll be able to get some great photos of wildlife. The trail is open from dawn to dusk all year. Oh, and this place is a turtle heaven—more turtles out sunning themselves than I've seen anyplace else. Must be something in the water.

    The visitor center itself contains a wealth of interesting exhibits and info for both young and old, including the 20,000 gallon Oxbow and Delta Rivers aquariums containing a variety of fish that live in the murky, slow-moving waters of oxbow lakes and swamps. Oh yes, and you can even sit in a crop duster airplane and take an aerial tour of the delta! The center is closed on Mondays, but is open almost every other day of the year, except some holidays. There is always something going on at the center, including special programs

Star of the Alligater Theater (above); pair of turtles sunning themselves (below)

like "Boo In The Bayou" at Halloween. This center was built and is run using funds from the 1/8th cent sales tax—a great investment for all of us and future generations.

To reach the center take Hwy. 65B in Pine Bluff and turn north onto Convention Center Drive, then continue .9 mile and TURN RIGHT into the center.

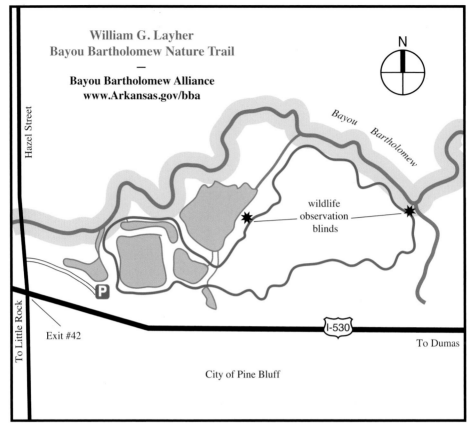

William G. Layher
Bayou Bartholomew Nature Trail
–
Bayou Bartholomew Alliance
www.Arkansas.gov/bba

N

Bayou Bartholomew

wildlife
observation
blinds

Hazel Street

To Little Rock

Exit #42

P

I-530

To Dumas

City of Pine Bluff

William G. Layher BAYOU BARTHOLOMEW NATURE TRAIL is a brand new trail in Pine Bluff that visits and showcases the longest bayou in the world (the bayou flows for 375 miles and has a million-acre watershed!). This easy and mostly level trail wanders through the forest and along the banks of the bayou where you can see cypress and tupelo swamps that are teaming with wildlife, including beaver and otters. My friend, Ken Eastin, who built this trail, told me that at one location some river otters kept messing up his trail each night by creating their "slide" across the trail where they played—look for this otter slide as you walk along, and if you spot the otters prepare to sit and be entertained! There are a couple of wildlife blinds located along the trail, and you'll find tons of waterfowl that stop in for a rest during the winter months. The trail is located right next to the interstate and makes a great stop whenever you are passing through Pine Bluff.

The bayou itself was named after Saint Bartholomew by French speaking Catholic settlers of the lower Mississippi River Valley—the bayou flows all the way down into Louisiana. Even though the water may be murky, it contains 117 species of fish, the second most diverse stream in all of North America!

To get to the trail take the Hazel Street exit (#42) off of I-530 in Pine Bluff, then go towards town just about 100 yards and TURN RIGHT onto a gravel drive and park at the end of the drive next to a pumping station building (UTM 590123E, 3781559N). The area is maintained by the Bayou Bartholomew Alliance, a non-profit organization that was created to help protect the bayou.

Cypress trees along the bayou (above);
baby otter (below)

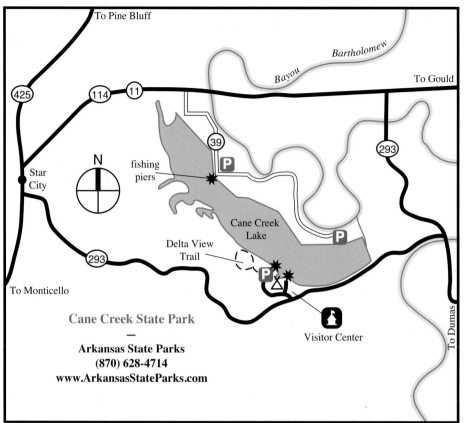

To Pine Bluff

Bartholomew

Bayou

To Gould

425   114   11

N

Star City

fishing piers

39

P

Cane Creek Lake

P

293

Delta View Trail

P

To Monticello

Cane Creek State Park
—
**Arkansas State Parks
(870) 628-4714
www.ArkansasStateParks.com**

Visitor Center

To Dumas

CANE CREEK STATE PARK has one main claim to fame that draws many visitors every year—about half of the lake surface is covered with an explosion of giant water lily blooms that create a stunning scene. Bring your own boat or rent a kayak and go drift around in the lilies for an unbelievable experience—it is really something! Oh yes, they also have a hiking and biking trail, fishing piers, RV rentals, a visitor center, and lots of wildlife and other wildflowers to see, plus a friendly park staff that has birding and kayak tours and other programs. The 1675-acre Cane Creek Lake is filled with dead timber that holds a lot of fish, so the fishing is great. Did I mention the water lilies that cover the lake that you can float around in? The best time for the lilies is late May, but give the park a call before you visit to see how they are progressing. There is also a gravel county road around the back (north) side of the park that goes to a fishing pier, a boat launch near the dam, and boat access to the cypress-filled Bayou Bartholomew swamp that winds through the area.

    To get to the state park, take Hwy. 293 east out of Star City for five miles and TURN LEFT into the park.

Water lilies cover Cane Creek Lake in the early summer

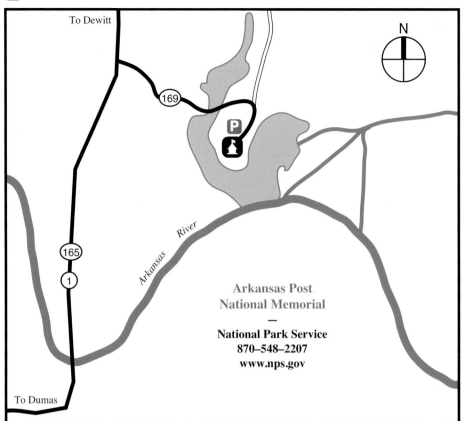

ARKANSAS POST NATIONAL MEMORIAL is perhaps the most scenic historical park in the state. Not being much of a history buff, I tend to avoid parks like this, but much to my surprise and delight I found a lot of really scenic stuff at this park, including backwater areas of the Arkansas River, hiking trails that wander through giant hardwood trees, and an abundance of bird life—especially great egrets that I have photographed frequently at the park. In the early summer the waterways are rimmed with impressive blooms of water hyacinths, an invasive plant originally from South America that seems right at home here and really adds a splash of color to the landscape. There seem to be deer everywhere, not to mention bald eagles and an occasional alligator. Naturalists Thomas Nuttall and John James Audubon spent time here and documented the area in the 1800's, so it has had a rich natural heritage for a long time. As usual the best times for viewing nature here are at the beginning and end of the day, however the gates to this park don't open until 8am, so you might need to park outside of the gates and hike in (the gates close at dark).

Oh yes, and there really is a great deal of interesting history to enjoy. Henri de Tonti established a trading post here in 1686 as one of the first permanent settlements in the lower Mississippi Valley. The trails wander around and visit locations of the old townsites and you can read up on the history at many spots along the way, as well as inside the visitor center. It is pretty neat to be able to stand right there in the middle of all that history.

To reach the park take Hwy. 165 south out of DeWitt or north out of Dumas, and turn east on Hwy. 169 for two miles to the park (about five miles north of the Arkansas River). There is no camping.

Water hyacinth at sunrise

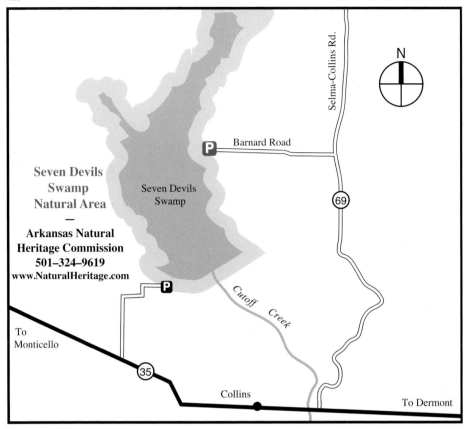

SEVEN DEVILS SWAMP NATURAL AREA is perhaps my most favorite swamp in the state. I can't exactly put my finger on why, but it is a magical place that will draw you in and keep you coming back again and again. You will need a canoe or kayak to visit this swamp, but once you push off from the boat ramp you will instantly be right out in the middle of it all, surrounded by a dense forest of cypress and tupelo trees both above and below you (great reflections!). The swamp is home to many species of birds and other wildlife, and I believe there is an active bald eagle nest in there somewhere. There are several "marked" canoe trails that penetrate this vast swamp, but it is good to just paddle around wherever your dreams take you and then head back when it is time to go home. I highly recommend you take along a GPS to help you find your way back to the boat ramp though—it is easy to get lost and confused out there.

There are a couple of access points into the swamp, but here is how to get to the one I like: From Monticello, go east on Hwy. 35 14 miles to Collins. From the Cut-off Creek Bridge go another .1 mile and TURN LEFT onto gravel CR#69 (Selma-Collins Road). Go north on this road for 3.6 miles and TURN LEFT onto Barnard Road, which will end at the boat ramp in 1.5 miles (UTM 631842E, 3715783N). The natural area is inside the Seven Devils Swamp Wildlife Management Area (Game and Fish Commission land), and is co-managed by both Game and Fish and the Arkansas Natural Heritage Commission. There are no facilities, but you are allowed to camp. Oh yes, and watch out for alligators!

Evening on the water in the swamp (above);
an alligater waits for you (below)

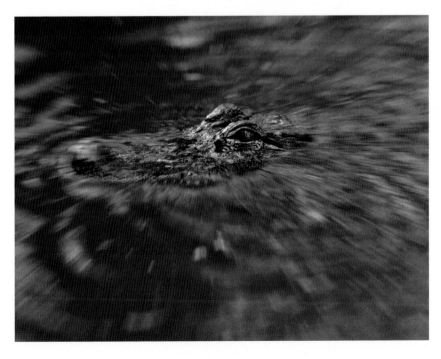

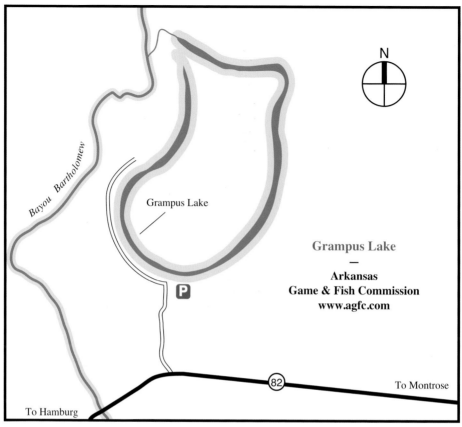

N

Bayou Bartholomew

Grampus Lake

P

Grampus Lake
—
**Arkansas
Game & Fish Commission
www.agfc.com**

82 To Montrose

To Hamburg

GRAMPUS LAKE is the first location I ever took genuine swamp photos at, and is an easy spot to get to where you will find a beautiful cypress swamp right outside your car window. Two things that make this swamp so neat to me are the "Spanish moss" that hangs from the cypress trees (actually it is a bromeliad in the pineapple family—but what the heck is that?), and all the duckweed that often covers the surface of the water in the summer and fall (a small bright green plant that floats on the water surface). It is possible to see much of the swamp by simply walking around the edge of the lake, but if you have a boat you can really get in and have a good look. You can view both sunrise and sunset through the swamp here. Springtime at this swamp is great, summer is wonderful, and fall is terrific! The lake is owned by the Arkansas Game and Fish Commission and you are allowed to fish, but there is no camping.

To get to the lake take Hwy. 82 west from Montrose (located on Hwy. 165 south of Dermott and west of Lake Chicot) and go 3.5 miles, then TURN RIGHT at the sign. Go .8 mile and the gravel road will end right at the boat ramp (UTM 634707E, 3686735N).

Grampus Lake swamp from the shore (above);
duckweed and fall color (below)

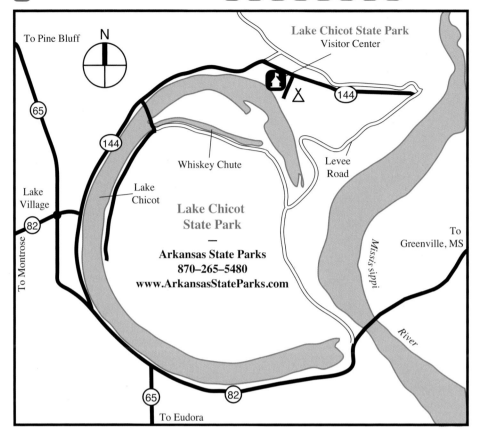

LAKE CHICOT STATE PARK is located on the largest oxbow lake in the US, which is also the largest natural lake in all of Arkansas. (An oxbow lake is a body of water that was once part of a main river channel that has been cut off from the river.) The park itself is located in a grove of majestic wild pecan trees (a great camping spot!), and has a hiking trail, visitor center, rental cabins, marina with boat rentals, and interpretive tours both on and off the water. Besides the cypress trees that line the lake, you can take a driving tour around the backside of the lake and along the levee road and see thick groves of cypress trees (along the "Whiskey Chute"), as well as lots of wildlife, including tons of birds. I love to get up early and motor or paddle around as the sun is rising—or in the evening when it is going down. This is a terrific spot for sunrise and sunset photos. This park has a wonderful, laid back feel to it, so plan to spend some time here and get to know the place.

    To get to the park, take Hwy. 144 northeast out of Lake Village for about 8 miles. Stop by the visitor center and get a map for the driving tour, and ask about evening cruises and other programs they offer.

Cypress trees just before sunrise at the edge of the lake

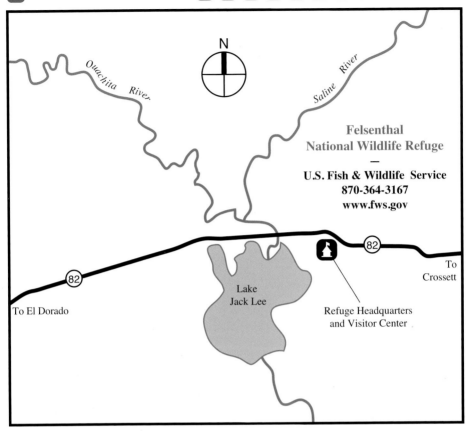

FELSENTHAL NATIONAL WILDLIFE REFUGE has always been a great hunting spot, but has some terrific wildlife watching and boating opportunities as well. Much of the refuge is flooded in the winter and is filled with thousands of waterfowl, and countless other species stop in for a rest during spring and fall migrations, including lots of songbirds, shorebirds, and wading birds. Lots of bald eagles too. But the king of the nearly 300 species of birds here (including almost 100 species that nest here!) are the resident red-cockaded woodpeckers, an endangered species. These small birds prefer the wide-open pine forests for nesting, and this is one of the few places in the region where you might actually have a chance to spot one. Stop by the visitor center (sadly, not open on weekends, so you may need to call during the week) and ask where to find the birds—there are also some great educational exhibits inside. There are several hiking trails on the refuge, including a paved trail at the visitor center, and a complex of short, easy trails at the Crossett Harbor RV Park area near the refuge office (some of the trails will be closed during November deer season, or in periods of high water). Oh yes, there are alligators too! Also the refuge is being stocked with black bears from the White River National Wildlife Refuge so be on the lookout. In the early summertime the Ouachita River and lakes on the refuge are lined with giant lotus blooms that compliment the cypress trees they often grow around.

The refuge is located between Crossett and Strong along Hwy. 82.

Lotus flowers and cypress on the Ouachita River (above); black bear (inset)

The Big Woods Region

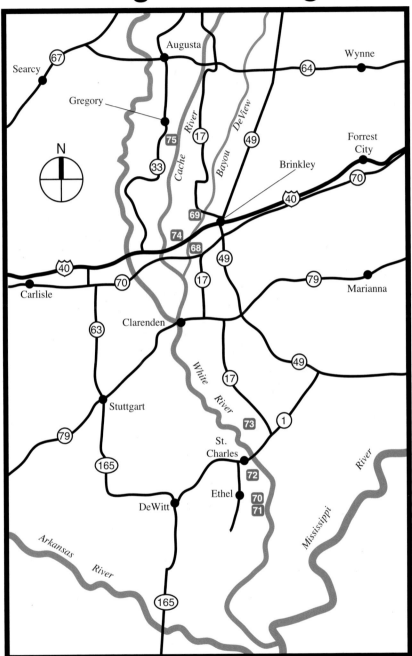

THE BIG WOODS REGION of eastern Arkansas is a major modern conservation success story, one that is not over, but is looking pretty good. Bottomland hardwood forest wetlands once numbered more than 8 million acres in Arkansas, but were doomed to be drained and cut for croplands, and the rivers torn up by channelization. The 1980's saw the beginning of a partnership between government agencies, private corporations, and conservation organizations, with The Nature Conservancy leading the way. Since then, more than 550,000 acres have been saved and protected within two federal and four state-owned management areas, collectively known as The Big Woods. In the middle of it all came the rediscovery of the Ivory-billed woodpecker in 2004, the holy grail of endangered species long thought to be extinct. Since that time, an extensive effort has been ongoing to locate a viable population of the birds, and as this book is going to press none have been found—but there is hope. As long as The Big Woods remains protected you will have the chance to view one of these rare and magnificent birds anytime you visit (learn more about the Ivory-bill rediscovery and search at www.nature.org/ivorybill).

And that is just the tip of the iceberg. Not only are The Big Woods a major environmental love story, but the place is crammed full of some of the most incredible cypress-tupelo swamps on the planet, with trees more than 1,000 years old, including one cypress that measures 43 feet in circumference! (And you can walk right up to this giant—thanks to the directions on page 166!) Having grown up in the mountains of northwest Arkansas, I never got to appreciate swamplands that much until I started doing research for this guidebook. And now I am in love with The Big Woods, and plan many trips there in the future—not to look for "Elvis" (the code word given to the Ivory-billed woodpecker during the early and secret search efforts), but to photograph the big trees and paddle my kayak out into the swamps for sunrise and sunset.

The Big Woods include the Cache River National Wildlife Refuge, Rex Hancock Black Swamp Wildlife Management Area, Dagmar Wildlife Management Area, and the White River National Wildlife Refuge, plus two smaller natural areas—Cache River Natural Area and Benson Creek Natural Area, both owned by the Arkansas Natural Heritage Commission.

There are many access points throughout The Big Woods, with a number of ATV trails that have been designated as special "birding" trails where foot travel is welcome. But to really see these places you need a boat. I have selected eight of my favorite locations for this section, but there are dozens more. You can find tons of info on the web (each agency has maps and location info available online), but you really should plan a visit to the White River Visitor Center at St. Charles (they are open on weekends too!).

One note about closures: some parts of The Big Woods may be closed from time to time for Ivory-billed woodpecker research, and also much of the White River Wildlife Refuge is closed in the winter annually (80%-90% of this 160,000-acre refuge is flooded each winter, so the roads are underwater). Be sure to check with the specific agency before visiting these areas for the latest data. And if you just happen to spot an Ivory-bill, give me a call!

Scenic Areas in The Big Woods Region

68

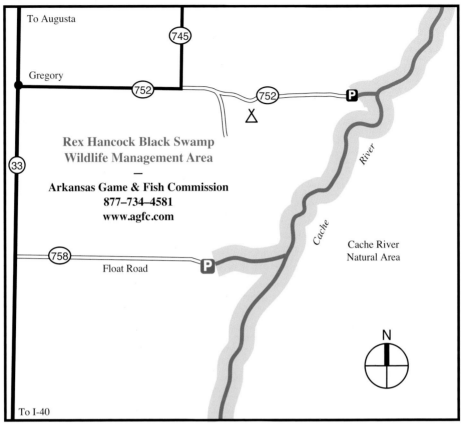

Rex Hancock BLACK SWAMP WILDLIFE MANAGEMENT AREA is located in the northern part of The Big Woods and lies within the general boundary of the Cache River National Wildlife Refuge (what a mouthful!). A large part of this swamp is protected as the Cache River Natural Area. I love the name Black Swamp, but what I like even more is paddling through the cypress swamps that run along the Cache River in this area. There are a number of access points, but my favorite is the lower access point at the end of Float Road that will put you into the southern part of the swamp. You can paddle around and explore the natural area upstream all you like, then turn around and float back. Or when the water is up in the late spring and early summer, you can float around through the dense swamps and not even make it out to the river. (You could also run a shuttle and float between the two access points described here.) Besides the beautiful trees all around, there are lots of waterfowl and other critters to see, especially in the wintertime.

    To reach the access point from the community of Gregory (from I-40 take exit 202 and travel north on Hwy. 33), go south on Hwy. 33 for 1.5 miles and TURN LEFT (east) onto CR#758/Float Road and follow it 1.8 miles to where it ends at the boat ramp (UTM 653857E, 3888564N). If the water is really low, you may need to drive up to the northern access point—take paved CR#752 on the south end of Gregory to the east for 1.4 miles, then continue to the RIGHT on CR#752 (CR#745 curves to the left at this intersection). Stay left on CR#752 past a primitive camping area and the road will end at the boat ramp (UTM 655922E, 3891014N)—a water canal will take you out to the Cache River. For info on the nearby Cache River National Wildlife Refuge, be sure to stop by their office that is located right on Hwy. 33 about 6 miles south of Gregory.

154

A quiet moment in the swamp

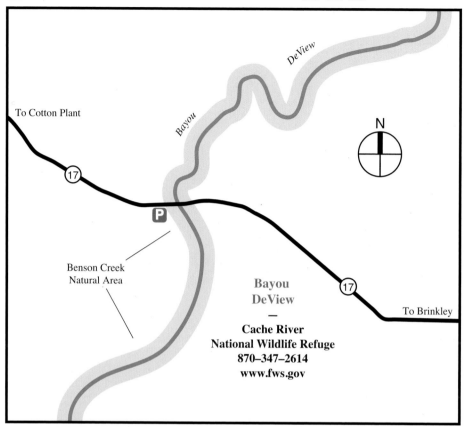

BAYOU DEVIEW, in the Cache River National Wildlife Refuge, was ground zero where the first confirmed sighting and rediscovery of the Ivory-billed woodpecker happened in February, 2004. The large bird that was thought to have been extinct for 60 years was sighted numerous times in this area during the following year of secret searching by various conservation organizations and government agencies. And while you are not likely to run into any of these "Holy Grail" of the endangered species birds in the bayou, you will see some beautiful swamp country, and probably a lot of woodpeckers too. You will need a canoe or kayak to visit this part of the bayou, but the access is easy and you won't have to paddle very far to see some really nice stuff. The Ivory-bills were sighted a little ways downstream from this Hwy. 17 access point, although there was activity both above and below the bridge. When you first put into the water, you are in a small tupelo-and-cypress-lined lake, but once you go either up or downstream for 1/4 mile or so, you will get into the narrow passages of the bayou and will find some pretty terrific ancient cypress trees.

To get to the access point, take I-40 exit #216 at Brinkley and go north on Hwy. 49, then TURN LEFT onto Hwy. 17 and go about three miles—the parking area is on the far end of the bridge to the left (UTM 660680E, 3867113N). And while most of this area is within the Cache River National Wildlife Refuge, 300 acres of the area on river-right (west side) is part of the Benson Creek Natural Area that is owned and managed by the Arkansas Natural Heritage Commission. During higher water, you can float from this point on downstream into the Dagmar Wildlife Management Area for even more great birding and swamp scenery (see next listing).

Cypress trees in Bayou DeView (above);
my photo of the elusive extinct bird that I made on April 1st this year (below)

Ivory-billed woodpecker information: www.nature.org/ivorybill

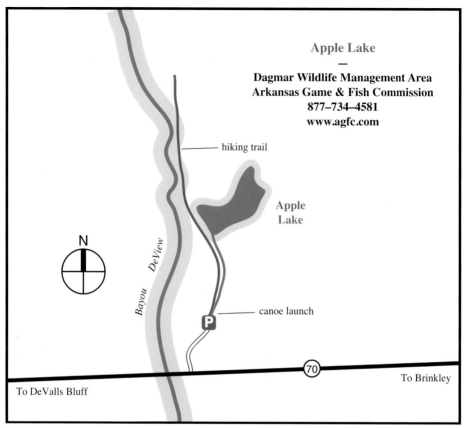

Apple Lake

—

Dagmar Wildlife Management Area
Arkansas Game & Fish Commission
877–734–4581
www.agfc.com

hiking trail

Apple
Lake

N

Bayou DeView

canoe launch

P

70

To Brinkley

To DeValls Bluff

APPLE LAKE, in the Dagmar Wildlife Management Area, is another favorite classic swamp location of mine, with the added flavor of being able to hike along one end of the lake so you don't always need a boat. It is a terrific place to watch the sunrise over the lake in the late spring and early summer. I've spent many early mornings in my canoe out in the middle of this small lake quietly watching the eastern sky and the water surface light up as the sun arrives. This is one lake that has lots of cypress and tupelos out in the middle instead of just lining it, and you are right in the thick of it all in just a .2 mile paddle from the boat launch ramp. The hiking trail that runs across a levee along the lake and the boat ramp both begin at the same location. When there is enough water, there is also an access point there where you can put your canoe in the water on the left side of the levee and paddle on into Bayou DeView, which is another canoe trail in this Dagmar Wildlife Management Area that is managed by the Arkansas Game and Fish Commission. You can also visit parts of Bayou DeView at the far end of the hiking trail, which is a one-way trail with a roundtrip of 1.5 miles. There is another great canoe trail and scenic drive nearby—see the next listing for that info.

The Apple Lake access is located between Brinkley and DeValls Bluff, off of Hwy. 70. From I-40 take exit #202 and go south on Hwy. 33, then TURN LEFT onto Hwy. 70 and go 7.5 miles, then TURN LEFT into the access area and park at the end of the road (UTM 657078E, 3856605N).

Early morning light on cypress and tupelo trees

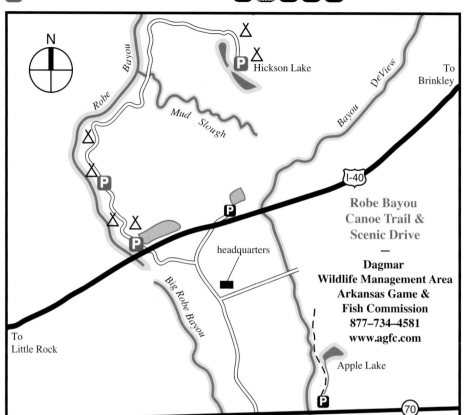

ROBE BAYOU CANOE TRAIL and SCENIC DRIVE is in the Dagmar Wildlife Management Area and is both a great canoe trail and also a wonderful short scenic drive. There are several great camping areas along the way as well, some where the bayou wraps around the camping area, so you'll have great views up and down the bayou without even getting out of the tent! (No facilities at these camping areas—just open ground to pitch your tent or park your RV on.) The bayou is lined with great cypress trees as it twists and turns into the heart of Dagmar Wildlife Management Area. If paddling a canoe, you can take your time and float silently around the bends and see all sorts of wildlife including herons and great egrets and perhaps a bald eagle or two. If making the trip in a car, you will be able to see much of the bayou from the road, and will be able to continue on to Hickson Lake where the road ends. This small lake has lots of great swamp trees around it, and is a perfect spot to launch your canoe for more exploration. All of this area is within a stone's throw of the ground zero Ivory-billed woodpecker location, so always be on the lookout for the next historical sighting! Like all of the swamp areas, visit early and late in the day for the best light, reflections, and wildlife movements.

To get to the Robe Bayou Canoe Trail from I-40, take either exit #202 and go south on Hwy. 33 to Biscoe and then TURN LEFT onto Hwy. 70 and go 7.0 miles and TURN LEFT at the management area sign (gravel road); or take exit #216 at Brinkley and head west on Hwy. 70 and then TURN RIGHT at the management area sign. From there follow the gravel road and bear left at the management area headquarters, then TURN LEFT at the next fork and you will begin the canoe trail and scenic drive just after you pass under I-40 (UTM 653940E, 3858965N). You can also continue on this road to the

Cypress trees line the bayou (above); great blue heron hunts for breakfast (below)

next put-in spot if you want to get away from the interstate noise. This is a good gravel road for any vehicle, and it is almost five miles back to the end of the road at Hickson Lake (UTM 655550E, 3861981N).

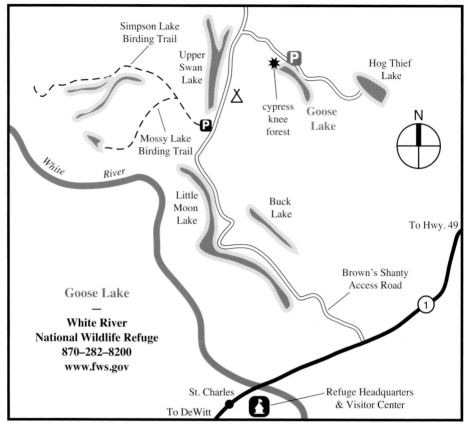

GOOSE LAKE, in the White River National Wildlife Refuge, is one place I had been looking for for many years—big cypress trees with a forest of interesting "knees" all around. What I do is wade out into the knees and set up my tripod just before dawn. As the swamp comes to life, not only does the light create some wonderful scenes, but there seems to always be wildlife prowling about both up in the trees and down in the water. The forest of knees are located right next to the road, just as you first get to Goose Lake, which is a small lake to begin with. I'm sure they are underwater much of the winter, and I like to go in the late spring and fall seasons for the best photos, although summertime is great too. Keep in mind that 80%–90% of this 160,000-acre refuge is flooded in the winter months and most of the refuge is closed off from December until the end of February. The roads may be closed anytime the water levels rise in the White River—best to always check the refuge web page and/or give them a call for current conditions before you make a long trip. Watch out for snakes!

To reach Goose Lake from the refuge headquarters at St. Charles, take Hwy. 1 east for 1.5 miles, over the White River bridge and TURN LEFT (north) at the Brown's Shanty Access sign (and pickup a brochure/permit at the billboard if you don't already have one). Follow this road for 3.6 miles and TURN RIGHT at the Goose Lake/Hog Thief Lake sign and continue another .5 mile and you will begin to see the upper end of the lake with the forest of knees on the right—park here (UTM 673201E, 3809608N). You can also view these knees and large cypress trees from the bank if you don't want to get wet. If you go back out on the main gravel road and continue on into the refuge, you will pass several turnoffs to other lakes and follow along some nice bayous with chances to view wildlife. You can

Goose Lake cypress trees (above); and the forest of knees (below)

also hike the birding trails to Simpson and Mossy Lakes (ATV trails that are level and easy to walk on). There are many ATV trails throughout the refuge and many of them have been labeled as special birding trails—check with the refuge office for maps to the trails, or you can also download them from their web page. Sound recordings and other Ivory-billed woodpecker data were taken at many places in the refuge, and with the vast acreage and prime habitat here, I suspect this is where our once-extinct bird is hiding.

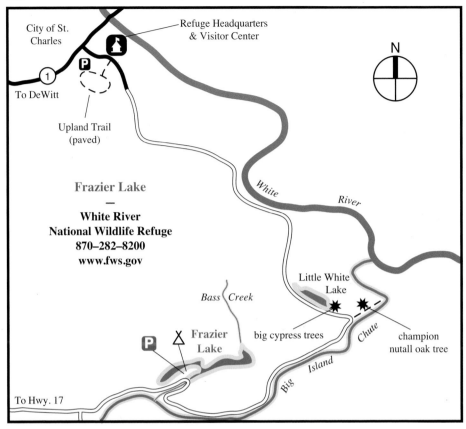

City of St.
Charles

To DeWitt

Refuge Headquarters
& Visitor Center

Upland Trail
(paved)

Frazier Lake
—
White River
National Wildlife Refuge
870–282–8200
www.fws.gov

White

River

Bass \ Creek

Little White
Lake

Frazier
Lake

big cypress trees

Chute

Big Island

champion
nutall oak tree

To Hwy. 17

N

FRAZIER LAKE, in the White River National Wildlife Refuge, is where many of the cypress swamp photos you've seen published were taken. There is a good reason for that—it is easy to get to and there are tons of great photo opportunities there. It is one of only a few lakes in the area that has cypress trees growing right out in the middle of the lake instead of just lining the banks. And it has some great views looking both east and west, so you can see the sunrise and sunset. You can see many of the neat cypress trees right from the bank, but as with most of the lakes in this region, you will find many more great things to explore if you put a boat in the water and paddle around. This is one of many lakes in the refuge where you are allowed to camp, but like all the rest there are no facilities of any kind. Unlike most of the other lakes in the refuge, this one is actually not a natural lake—a small dam across Bass Creek forms the lake. NOTE: this area is closed to all entry from November 1st until the end of February, and also at any time the water levels get too high in the refuge. Call the refuge (number is on the map above) at any time to get an updated message about road conditions (answered 24/7).

To get to Frazier Lake (UTM 673320E, 3800122N), first stop in at the refuge visitor center just south of Hwy. 1 at the edge of St. Charles—this is where you need to begin any visit to the refuge, and it is open year-round, including weekends! They have some great exhibits there and a short movie that will explain a lot of what the refuge is all about. Volunteers from the Friends of White River run the bookstore and do a lot of great stuff for the refuge.

To get to the lake from the visitor center, continue on into the refuge. You will pass Little White Lake on the left at 3.1, and at the far end of it there are some very large

Sunrise through the cypress trees on Frazier Lake

cypress trees right next to the road. When the water is low you can walk in among these giants and it makes you feel very small. Just beyond that point, where the road makes a hard turn to the right, there is a small trail off to the left that will take you to the state champion Nuttall Oak tree. You will come to Frazier Lake 5.3 miles past the visitor center. You can also get to Frazier Lake from the back side, but you miss all the neat stuff along the way. From the visitor center TURN LEFT onto Hwy. 1 (towards DeWitt) and TURN LEFT onto Hwy. 17 after 1.4 miles, then go 3.0 miles and TURN LEFT at the Frazier Lake Access sign (gravel road). Stay on this road for 1.5 miles and you will enter the refuge, then it is another .8 mile to Frazer Lake.

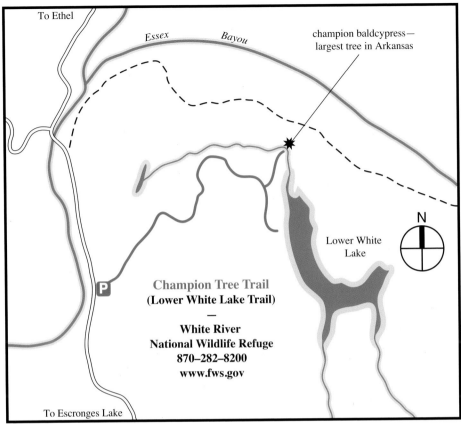

To Ethel

Essex Bayou

champion baldcypress—
largest tree in Arkansas

N

Lower White Lake

P

Champion Tree Trail
(Lower White Lake Trail)
—
White River
National Wildlife Refuge
870–282–8200
www.fws.gov

To Escronges Lake

CHAMPION TREE TRAIL, in the White River National Wildlife Refuge, is also the trail to Lower White Lake. Not only will you find a beautiful lake that is lined with large cypress trees at the end of this one mile ATV trail, but the trail also leads to the largest cypress tree in Arkansas, which just so happens to also be the largest tree in Arkansas, and also the largest living thing in Arkansas! In fact it is one of the largest trees in about 40 of the 50 United States, and is a real beauty of a tree as well. You will see and admire many giant cypress trees in this refuge, but it literally does tower above all the rest at 120' tall, with a circumference of 43 FEET! Champion trees are ranked using a combination of the DBH (diameter breast high—4.5 feet high), the height, and the width of the crown, along with a standard formula to arrive at the "bigness factor." This incredible tree has a bigness factor of 645, with the next largest tree species in Arkansas being "only" 461. Some of the knees for this tree are nearly ten feet tall, and it is surrounded by dozens of knees. Stand at the base of this monster and just admire it—the largest living thing in Arkansas, wow! (www.forestry.state.ar.us/education/education.html)

     To get to the trailhead from St. Charles, go west on Hwy. 1 about a mile and TURN LEFT (south) onto Hwy. 17 for about six miles. TURN LEFT at the Ethel Access sign (paved), then follow the paved road and TURN RIGHT onto Bisswanger Road after 1.4 miles (still paved). TURN LEFT onto Refuge Road after another 1.4 miles (also paved), then you will come to the refuge entrance after 1.0. TURN RIGHT on the gravel road and head into the refuge (pick up a brochure there). Drive 1.3 miles and TURN LEFT at the fork, crossing Essex Bayou, then continue on .5 mile to a pulloff on the LEFT and park (this is 1.8 miles from the entrance and is now marked with a Champion

The largest living thing in Arkansas!

Tree Trail sign). Follow the wide and level ATV trail about 1.0 mile to a marked intersection and TURN LEFT (if you went straight ahead there the trail ends at scenic Lower White Lake). Follow the trail to the left and it will end at a nice wide bench—sit down and gaze up at the giant tree directly in front of you! (UTM 674415E, 3791094N) There are more giant cypress trees in the area to enjoy, but this is the *champion*.

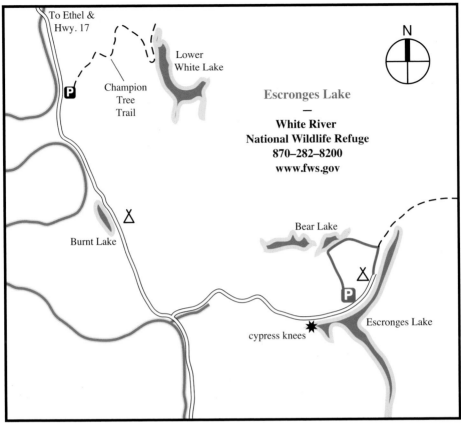

ESCRONGES LAKE, in the White River National Wildlife Refuge, is another beautiful lake in this vast refuge that has a lot of great cypress trees around it, along with an area crowded with cypress knees. I often find myself heading to this lake when the sun gets low on the western horizon. The light on the trees and reflections in the water is really nice. There is a campground area here, and also a couple of ATV trails for you to explore. One of the trails makes a loop and goes out to Bear Lake (UTM 676314E, 3788595N), and don't tell anyone that I told you, but I hear there is a bald eagle nest on this little lake, one of at least five active nests in the refuge. (The trail to the lake may be closed in the early spring due to the eagle nesting activity.) It is a short (.4 mile) trail to Bear Lake that begins just across the road from the campground area (UTM 676505E, 3787999N), and besides the eagle nest (which you probably cannot see due to the thick foliage), the lake is filled with cypress trees and is a beautiful little lake. Once you reach the lake, you can continue to the right on the yellow-painted ATV trail and loop back to Escronges Lake, for a total loop of 1.3 miles.

Speaking of bears, the White River Refuge is home to the last population of native black bears, several hundred of them in fact. The rest of the state was stocked with bears from Minnesota in the 1960's after the native population was all but wiped out. So if you happen to see a bear on the refuge, he won't have a Yankee accent!

To reach Escronges Lake from the Champion Tree Trail (see directions on the previous listing), continue on the gravel refuge road and go past Burnt Lake and then TURN LEFT at the fork and the road ends at Escronges Lake. Goodness, can you just imagine all of these hardwoods in the fall when they really start blazing? Remember that

Evening light on Escronges Lake (above); and a native black bear (below)

this area is generally closed from December through the end of February, and anytime there is high water in the White River—call the refuge for the latest information.

Southwest Region

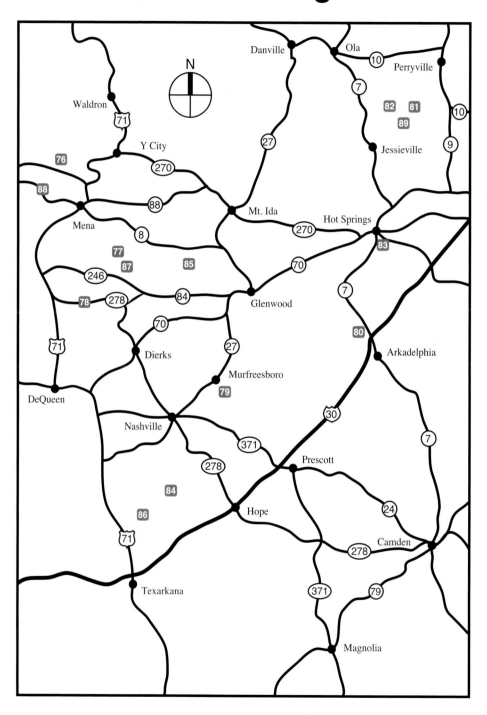

The SOUTHWEST REGION of Arkansas has a mix of spectacular mountain ranges—some of the tallest in the state—and flat prairie land where you'll find brilliant displays of wildflowers. It is also home to many beautiful rivers that run clear and deep, and one of the very best whitewater spots in the country. At the giant Millwood Lake, you'll find more birds than in just about any other area (plus a few alligators too). There are two scenic drives in this region—one being the best ridgetop drive in this part of the country, while the other winds through remote wilderness. There are mountaintops and waterfalls, and oh yes, a park where you can go hunt for diamonds and keep all that you find!

Scenic Areas in the Southwest Region

76

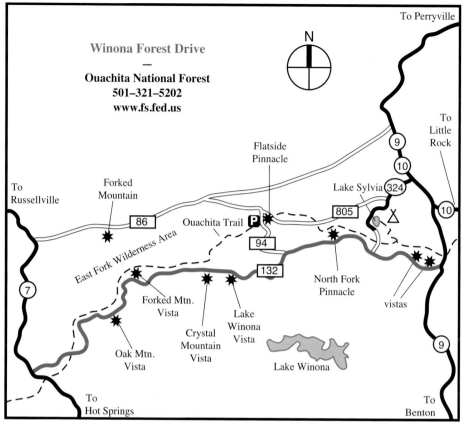

WINONA FOREST DRIVE is one of the great scenic auto tours in Arkansas. This good gravel road winds 25.7 miles through the heart of the Ouachita Mountains, between Hwy. 7 and Hwy. 9. There are numerous scenic vistas along the way, including a stop where you can climb up a mountain to an old fire tower site, and another location where you can dig for natural quartz crystals. It is a great trip at any time of the year, but a fall tour will reward you with some stunning autumn color (the color normally peaks in November). You can make this trip in either direction, but we'll begin from the Hwy. 9 side since it is the closest to Little Rock. (Or begin on Hwy. 7 six miles north of Jessieville and drive it in reverse.)

From Little Rock, take Hwy. 10 west out of town and TURN LEFT (south) on Hwy. 9. Go 3.2 miles and TURN RIGHT on FR#132 at the Winona Forest Drive sign—this is the beginning of the auto tour (zero your odometer there). At 1.0 mile there is a pulloff and vista where you can get a great shot of the sunrise over the distant Lake Maumelle. At 2.9 miles is the Nancy Mountain Vista, another great view out over the mountains. At 4.2 miles there is an intersection—a right turn will take you down to Lake Sylvia (great camping, swimming, and hiking area), and also to a historical Girl Scout camp from the 1930's, but we'll continue straight ahead. At 5.6 miles is a pulloff for a trail that leads .5 mile UP the hill to North Fork Pinnacle, where you will have some great views and find the foundation of an old fire lookout tower (UTM 513578E, 3857292N, topo map says 1,515' elevation). At 8.3 miles there is an intersection with FR#94—continue LEFT for the auto tour (FR#94 goes over to Flatside Pinnacle—see the next listing). At 11.1 miles is the Lake Winona Vista, and at 11.7 miles is a turnoff to Crystal Mountain

The view of Forked Mountain from Forked Mountain Vista (above); quartz crystals free for the taking (below)

Vista. This is a ROUGH road with sharp rocks up to the top (UTM 505782E, 3854891N), and it is best to get out and hike it. The unique thing here is that there are veins of natural quartz crystals scattered around the mountain in the sandstone boulders and rock outcrops near the road, and you are allowed to hunt and keep any that you find!

At 17.3 miles is the turnout with the best view of all, looking out over the Flatside Wilderness to my favorite mountain in the state, Forked Mountain (see listing later in this book). The final vista is Oak Mountain Vista, where you'll find a great sunrise view in the winter. You come out to smooth road and Hwy. 7 at 25.7 miles.

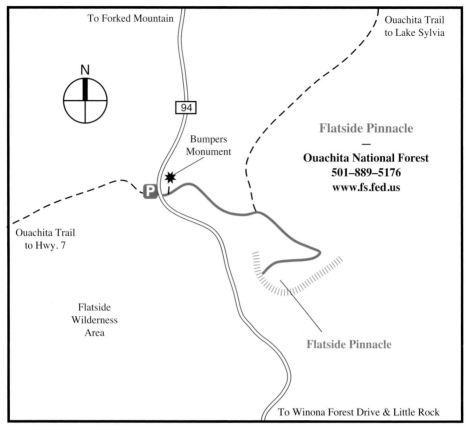

To Forked Mountain

Ouachita Trail
to Lake Sylvia

N

94

Bumpers
Monument

Flatside Pinnacle
—
**Ouachita National Forest
501–889–5176
www.fs.fed.us**

P

Ouachita Trail
to Hwy. 7

Flatside
Wilderness
Area

Flatside Pinnacle

To Winona Forest Drive & Little Rock

FLATSIDE PINNACLE is located along the Ouachita Trail just off of the Winona Forest Drive and is a pretty easy hike to get on top of from the parking area. Once up there, you will find a commanding view of not only the 9,507-acre Flatside Wilderness Area, but also much of the surrounding forest, as rows upon rows of forested ridgetops just seem to go on forever. I believe this to be the finest view in all of the Ouachitas, and one of the very best in this part of the country. It is a great spot for photos of the sunset, and if you are an early riser, you can also see the sunrise from up on top as well. The USGS topo map has it listed at over 1,500' tall (UTM 508188E, 3858760N).

To get to the parking area, follow the directions for the Winona Forest Drive (previous pages) until you come to FR#94 at the 8.3 mile mark, then TURN RIGHT onto FR#94 and continue for 2.9 miles and park at the trailhead. The Ouachita Trail crosses the road here, and you will hike on this trail for most of the way—follow it up the hillside. If you look closely after about 100 feet of hiking, you will find a faint trail that goes off to the left—it leads to a stone marker that recognizes Senator Dale Bumpers for his outstanding service over the years to help protect wilderness areas in Arkansas. He was one of our best politicians ever, and my dog, Aspen, and I were here when this monument was dedicated—in fact Aspen ran up to the Senator and nipped his arm! There are similar stone monuments placed at the edge of each national forest wilderness area in Arkansas. OK, back to the hike.

The trail winds on up the hill to a level spot, or "saddle," where the Ouachita Trail turns back to the left, but you want to TURN RIGHT and continue through a primitive camp area and keep going on up the hill. The trail switchbacks to the right and ends

The view from on top of Flatside Pinnacle (above, Forked Mtn. is in the upper right);
Dale Bumpers monument (below)

at the top edge of the mountain, a hike of .3 mile. The footing is not too good up there and the rocks are not very wide, so be extremely careful. The pointed mountain that you can see off in the distance is Forked Mountain, our next scenic location to visit. Sit down and enjoy the incredible view, then return to the trailhead by the same route.

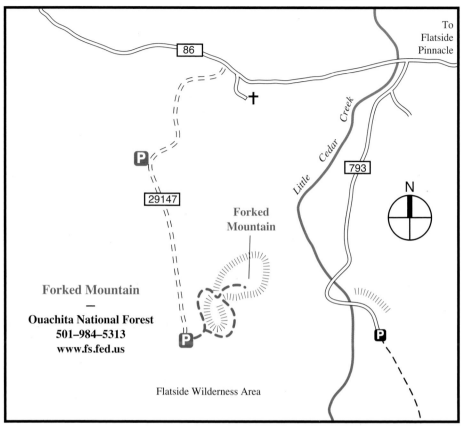

FORKED MOUNTAIN is my favorite mountain in Arkansas (1,350' tall). It reminds me more of a peak in the Rocky Mountains than in the Ouachitas. You can see views of it from spots along Hwy. 7, the Winona Forest Drive, and Flatside Pinnacle, but to really experience this mountain you just have to go climb it—one of the few mountains in Arkansas that requires a degree of skill to climb, which means it is not for the faint of heart or novice hiker! The view from on top is quite spectacular, but to me the biggest thrill is the *steep* climb up the giant boulder field to reach the summit. There are actually two peaks, the smaller one being completely tree-covered, but the larger peak has some open areas and great views.

To get to Forked Mountain (UTM 496145E, 3857689N), take FR#86 (gravel) east from Hwy. 7 for 4.0 miles and TURN RIGHT onto a paper company road #29147 (the turnoff on Hwy. 7 is located just south of Hollis, which is north of Jessieville). This paper company road goes steeply up the hill and dead-ends at the closest point to the mountain, however the road is in really bad shape and requires a serious high-clearance 4wd vehicle. You may want to park your car after .3 mile and hike up to the end of the road. (You can also reach this turnoff from Flatside Pinnacle—continue north on FR#94 and TURN LEFT onto FR#86 and follow it six miles to the paper company road.)

Once you get to the parking area, hike up a little four-wheeler road towards the mountain, and then when you get to the top of this little road you have to decide if you are going up the boulder route or the forest route. The forest route is easier, but still very steep. For the forest route, just keep following the little road to the LEFT, but it will end soon, so just keep on hiking/bushwhacking across some boulders, through the woods as you gradu-

Forked Mountain (above); the boulder field below the summit (inset)

ally climb up towards your right. At some point you will be able to see where others have scrambled steeply up to the saddle in between both peaks—follow it on up to the saddle. Once standing in the saddle the big peak is UP to your left, and then you are on top of the world!

For the rock scramble route, go to the top of the little road from the parking area and head out into the woods around the RIGHT side of the mountain, and remain level until you come out to a large open boulder field, then simply turn LEFT and climb up hand over fist until you reach the saddle in between the two peaks. Careful now, and watch your step. Once up to the saddle, continue to climb up to the RIGHT and you will be on top. The views out over the wilderness are breathtaking (or was that the climb?), and you can see Flatside Wilderness spread out before you, as well as Flatside Pinnacle way off in the distance.

177

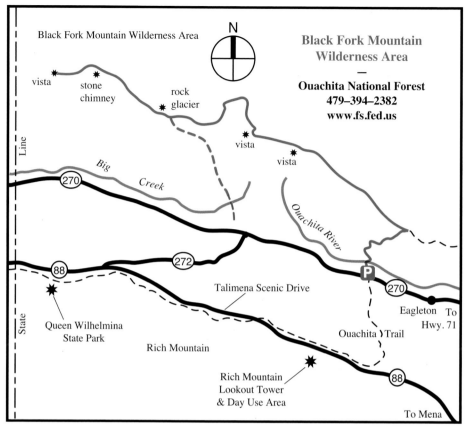

BLACK FORK MOUNTAIN WILDERNESS AREA doesn't get much traffic but has some really neat natural features including a grove of stunted, hundred year old oak trees and some really impressive rock "glaciers." There is a good hiking trail that will take you up onto the mountain, past the glaciers and to the grove of stunted oaks, and as an added bonus, there are some great views out across the Ouachita River Valley over to Rich Mountain. Most folks will want to backpack this trail and spend the night up on top of the mountain, but you can also make a dayhike out of it (mountain bikes are not allowed in the 7,568-acre wilderness). This is a great hike to do in the wintertime or early spring.

    To get to the trailhead, go north on Hwy. 71 from Mena about six miles and turn west onto Hwy. 270, and the trailhead is located on the right about a mile past the community of Eagleton. Park there and begin your hike on the Ouachita Trail, and then TURN LEFT onto the Blackfork Mountain Trail after about a mile. The trail sort of peters out up on top after about six miles from the trailhead, and then you simply return the same way that you came in, or you can take an old mule trail back down the mountain and come out on the highway, then hike along it back to the trailhead to complete a loop of sorts.

One of the great rock "glaciers" on Black Fork Mountain

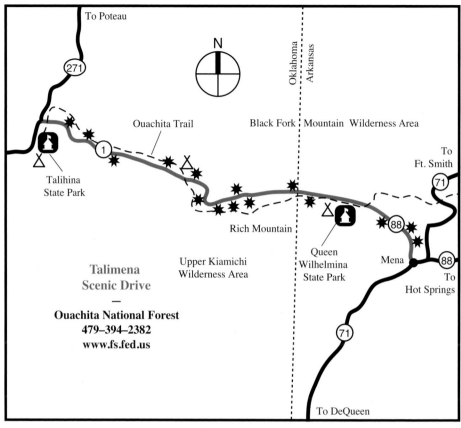

To Poteau

N

Oklahoma | Arkansas

271

Ouachita Trail

Black Fork Mountain Wilderness Area

To
Ft. Smith

1

71

Talihina
State Park

Rich Mountain

88

Mena

88

**Talimena
Scenic Drive**

—

**Ouachita National Forest
479–394–2382
www.fs.fed.us**

Upper Kiamichi
Wilderness Area

Queen
Wilhelmina
State Park

To
Hot Springs

71

To DeQueen

TALIMENA SCENIC DRIVE is one of the best scenic drives in the United States for sure, and you will see terrific views at just about every twist and turn of the road. This 54-mile National Scenic Byway begins at Mena, Arkansas, climbs up onto Rich Mountain and on past Queen Wilhelmina State Park, then eventually enters Oklahoma and continues on as Hwy. 1 through more dramatic vistas, ending at Hwy. 271 in Oklahoma. There are several hiking trails along the way, including the Ouachita National Recreation Trail, plus several shorter trails. There are 23 vistas and 15 historical sites along the drive. Did I mention the views were pretty darn spectacular? You don't have to go very far to find those incredible views—a great sunrise spot is right at the very first and second vistas, just a couple of miles past the start of the drive. There is an information station at either end of the drive where you can find out all sorts of neat things, and get more detailed information. Oh yes, and be on the lookout for bears—I almost always see a bear when I visit.

    To reach the beginning of the scenic drive, turn west onto Hwy. 88 in beautiful downtown Mena and head up the hill to the visitor center. Then roll down the windows and enjoy the scenery!

Sunset in the Ouachitas—the notch at the upper left is the scenic drive corridor (above); a pair of black bear cubs (below)

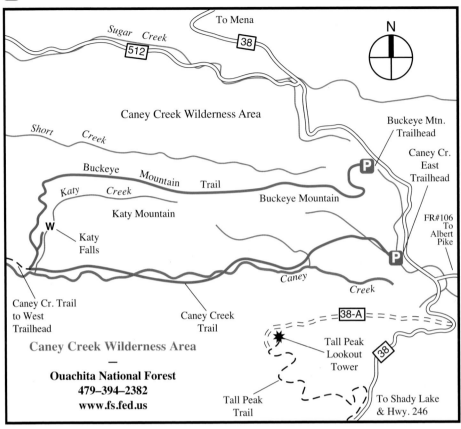

CANEY CREEK WILDERNESS AREA is the oldest wilderness area in Arkansas (1975), and contains the first backpacking trail that was built in the state.. Besides the beautiful Caney Creek that runs through the middle of the area, my favorite part of this wilderness is the Buckeye Mountain Trail, which is the Talimena Scenic Drive of hiking trails in Arkansas (is seems like there is a great scenic view around every corner!). You will see many great vistas along this ridgetop trail, and if you hike it early in the morning, the sunrise can be quite spectacular. You can connect both trails for a great weekend backpack loop, or just hike either trail as a dayhike. My normal hike is to begin early and hike in on the Buckeye Mountain Trail from FR#38, camp down along Caney Creek, then follow the Caney Creek Trail back to the same forest road, drop my pack in the woods, and hike the road up to my car to complete the loop. One note of caution—the Caney Creek Trail crosses the creek many times, so don't make this trip during high water. You can also hike the trail all the way through the wilderness area and exit on the western end after you cross the Cossatot River (again, don't attempt during high water).

     Besides the creek and the terrific views up high, there is also a neat waterfall near the junction of the two trails, up a side creek—Katy Falls (UTM 400716E, 3806487N). If you hike along the main creek in the summertime, you will see vast stretches of tall grasses growing in the big flat areas. The only other place I have seen this grass is up on top of Black Fork Mountain.

     To reach the trailheads from the south, take Hwy. 246 west from the community of Athens a couple miles and TURN RIGHT onto FR#38 (towards Shady Lake). Go past Shady Lake and later the turnoff to Tall Peak, and you will come to the East Caney

Sunrise from Buckeye Mountain (above); wildflowers along Caney Creek (right)

Creek Trailhead on your left at about seven miles. Continue on up the forest road another mile to the top of the hill and park on the LEFT at the Buckeye Mountain Trailhead (UTM 405525E, 3807747N), about eight miles from the highway.

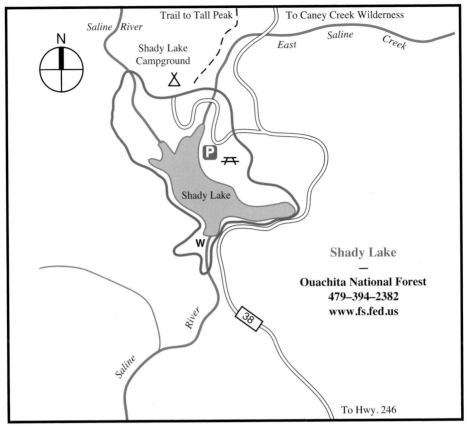

N

Saline River

Trail to Tall Peak

To Caney Creek Wilderness

Saline Creek

East

Shady Lake
Campground

P

Shady Lake

W

Shady Lake
—
**Ouachita National Forest
479–394–2382
www.fs.fed.us**

River

38

Saline

To Hwy. 246

SHADY LAKE is a neat little forest service lake tucked away in the mountains that has hiking trails, waterfalls, swimming area, and an all around good feel to it. This place is quiet and secluded and just beautiful. Parts of it were constructed by the Civilian Conservation Corps in the 1930's, and you can still see some of their fine stone workmanship. There is a loop trail that circles the lake (also open to mountain bikes), and a trail that climbs up to the top of Tall Peak. My favorite spot here is just below the dam of the lake (UTM 405485E, 3802202N)—the spillway and the boulder-strewn stream below it are wonderful. And it is a great lake to put a canoe in and paddle around—you won't be bothered by boats with big motors, as only electric motors are allowed.

To reach Shady Lake from the south, take Hwy. 246 west from the community of Athens a couple miles and TURN RIGHT onto FR#38, then it is three miles to Shady Lake—you will pass the spillway area first on your left.

Shady Lake looking towards Tall Peak (above);
the spillway (below)

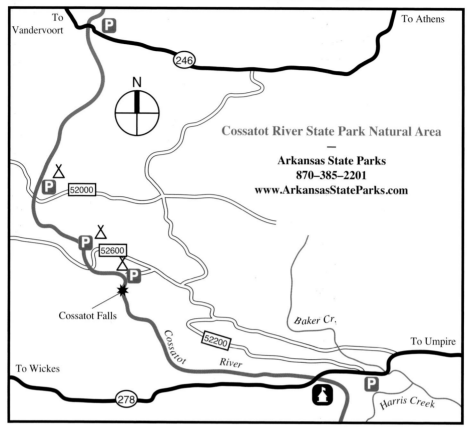

COSSATOT RIVER STATE PARK NATURAL AREA is well known as being a great whitewater kayaking spot, especially when the water is up, but Cossatot Falls is also one of the most scenic natural features in the state as well (UTM 387149E, 3798052N). It is an easy hike from the parking area to reach several locations along the cascade area known as Cossatot Falls, where you can watch all the whitewater action, or bring your camera and photograph the churning waters as they smooth down the boulders all along the way. Even when the water levels drop in the summertime, this is a terrific place to wander around and swim in some very nice deep pools.

On the civilized end of the park, there is a brand new multi-million dollar visitor center, right on Hwy. 278, that has a lot of neat exhibits and is well worth a stop at, even if you don't plan to drive into the middle of the park to see the falls area.

Besides all the whitewater rapids, there are also hiking trails in the park. One is the three-mile Harris Creek Loop Trail near the visitor center that visits a variety of habitats and has a great view of the river. On the upstream end of the park, at Hwy. 246, there is a short nature trail and wheelchair accessible bridge that looms over the river. Some day there will be a 14-mile long backpacking trail that follows the river from one end of the park to another. I designed and laid out this rugged trail many years ago, but the construction end of it has been very slow—ask at the visitor center about the progress. Camping is only allowed at the four camping areas along the river.

A kayaker in the "washing machine" at Cossatot Falls

The visitor center is located on Hwy. 278 between Umpire and Wickes, and the northern end of the park is along Hwy. 246 between Athens and Vandervoort. To reach Cossatot Falls there is a series of paper company gravel roads that will take you to it from either highway — just follow the signs.

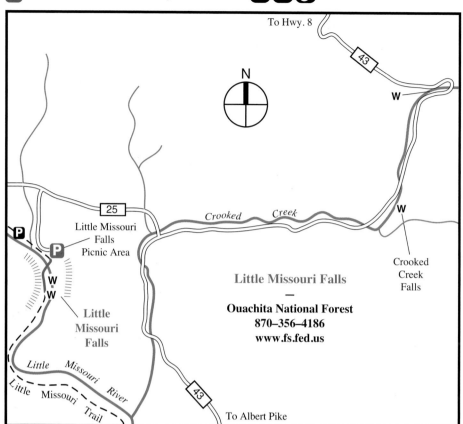

LITTLE MISSOURI FALLS is not a giant thundering waterfall, but rather a series of cascades that spill into pools of emerald water. These falls are quite beautiful, easy to get to, and attract a lot of visitors all year long (UTM 415592E, 389080N). The forest service recently built a large bridge across the river at the head of the waterfalls, making it possible to access the viewing areas even during periods of high water flow, when the cascades are really up and running. One of the lower pools is deep enough for swimming, and I've taken many dips on moonlit nights there while I was working on the Little Missouri Hiking Trail that runs through the recreation area and on downstream. When there is ample water—normally throughout the winter and springtime—the drive to this dayuse area can be quite scenic since the road runs along Crooked Creek, which has many cascades and waterfalls within view of the forest road.

To get to the falls from Langley (west from Glenwood on Hwy. 70 and then west on Hwy. 84), take Hwy. 369 six miles to Albert Pike Recreation Area. Continue straight through the campground as the road turns to FR#73 (gravel), and follow it about three miles and TURN LEFT onto FR#43. Go 4.3 miles to the intersection with FR#25 (you will have been driving through the Crooked Creek canyon for the past .5 mile—lots of nice cascades!). TURN LEFT onto FR#25 and go .7 mile and TURN LEFT at the big sign, which will take you down into the picnic area where you park. The paved trail takes off there and crosses the creek on the big bridge and goes to a pair of overlooks with good views of the cascade area. From Norman, take Hwy. 8 west 12.7 miles and TURN LEFT onto FR#43. Go 4.7 miles and TURN RIGHT on FR#25, then TURN LEFT after .7 mile to get to Little Missouri Falls.

Little Missouri Falls from the downstream end

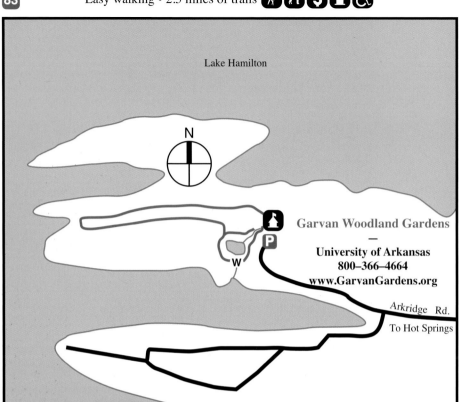

GARVAN WOODLAND GARDENS is a photographer's, flower lover's, and just plain lover's delight! Come explore over 40 acres of finely landscaped gardens that bloom all year long with hundreds of species of flowers, shrubs, trees, and gosh, just about anything and everything that blooms! You'll find many waterfalls and cascades spilling over scenic rockwork and into reflecting pools. (The waterfalls flow all year long!) There are 2.5 miles of trails that wind through the area, so you have plenty of access. The property is owned and operated by the University of Arkansas and there is an entrance fee, but you will get your money's worth in just a few minutes.

There is a small cafe on site, but here is a great idea for your next "date" with your significant other—take a picnic lunch with you and dine among the flowers in the garden—there are many great romantic spots all over the place.

Since different species bloom at different times, be sure to check their web page for "what's blooming" so you can plan your trip. Naturally spring and summer will be the best times, but there are also things blooming in the fall and winter too, and remember those waterfalls! Open every day but Thanksgiving, Christmas and New Year's.

To get to the gardens from the Hwy. 270 bypass around Hot Springs, take the Carpenter Dam Road exit (#7) and go 3.5 miles. TURN RIGHT onto Arkridge Road and go 1.0 mile to the entrance.

Tulips along the path

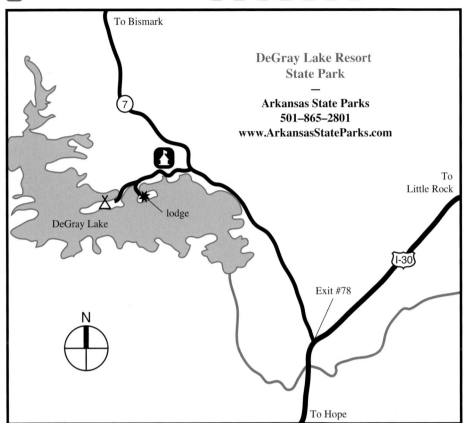

To Bismark

7

DeGray Lake Resort
State Park
—
Arkansas State Parks
501–865–2801
www.ArkansasStateParks.com

To
Little Rock

lodge

DeGray Lake

I-30

Exit #78

N

To Hope

DEGRAY LAKE RESORT STATE PARK is one of the more civilized and manicured of all our state parks, with a large lodge, golf course, tennis courts, a marina, and horseback riding stables. And while they have lots of camping areas and hiking trails, their main claim to fame in the natural world is the large number of bald eagles that live in the park during the winter time. The park staff conducts numerous barge tours to go look for eagles, and it is not uncommon to drift directly underneath one of these majestic birds. Oh yes, and the park staff also conducts a variety of other unique tours and programs during the year, including island snorkeling and kayak tours, hayrides, storytelling festivals, and moonlit cruises on the massive DeGray Lake. All in all, there is plenty of neat stuff for the entire family to do!

From a photographer's standpoint, you'll find lots of wading birds fishing around the edges of the lake, and there is a great sunrise and sunset spot from the very end of the park, just past the swimming area (nice sunsets from on top of the dam right along the main highway too).

To get to the park from I-30, take the Hwy. 7 exit (#78) and go north six miles; or from Hot Springs, go south on Hwy. 7 about 21 miles.

Bald eagle

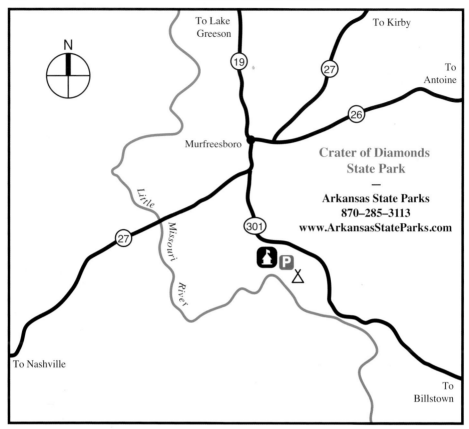

CRATER OF DIAMONDS STATE PARK is the only public place in the world where you can go look for diamonds and keep any that you find! And these are not dime-store diamonds, some of the 25,000 diamonds that have been found since the park was established in 1972 are worth millions. There are many other types of rocks and minerals found at the park too, including amethyst, agate, jasper, garnet, and quartz. Here's the deal: you pay an entrance fee, perhaps rent some digging tools, and then you are free to explore and dig all you like in the 37-acre field of diamond-bearing soil that is plowed periodically. Take anything you find to the newly opened Diamond Discovery Center and they will identify your treasure, then it is all yours to keep! This new center is a great place to learn how to best spend your time hunting for diamonds, and contains a great deal of history and other info about the park. I'll give you just one hint about all of this—don't go in the summertime since the dark soil can get really hot!

There are also hiking trails, a wildlife observation blind, camping, and a new 14,700 square foot water park where you can go to cool down if you visit in the summertime. Oh yes, and the Little Missouri River is nearby where you can catch a variety of fish including trout.

Murfreesboro is located south of Hot Springs, north of Hope, and west of Arkadelphia. To get to the park from Murfreesboro, take Hwy. 301 for 2.5 miles south to the park. Good luck, and send me any diamonds that you don't want to keep!

In the diamond field

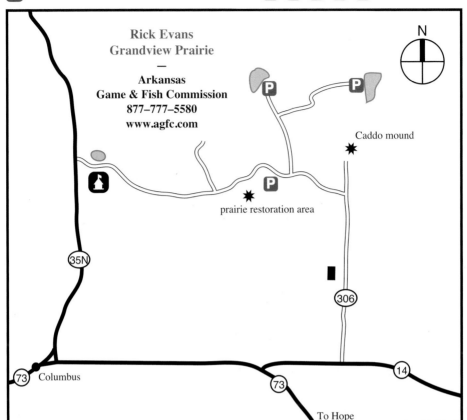

Rick Evans
Grandview Prairie
—
**Arkansas
Game & Fish Commission**
877–777–5580
www.agfc.com

N

Caddo mound

prairie restoration area

35N

306

73   Columbus

73

14

To Hope

Rick Evans GRANDVIEW PRAIRIE is the largest tract of protected blackland prairie in the nation at nearly 5,000 acres. It is owned by the Arkansas Game and Fish Commission and they operate both a Conservation Education Center and Wildlife Management Area there. There is abundant wildlife that can be seen all throughout the tract, however the main attraction here for me are the WILDFLOWERS! You can literally drive for three miles with fields of wildflowers on both sides of the road. Sometimes they may not look like much more than just an overgrown hay field, but stop anywhere you please and get out and walk around from early spring through fall and you will discover millions of wildflowers at your feet! There are also a couple of lakes that attract lots of wading birds; and deer, turkeys, and other game animals roam about. The office is open during the week, but it is not really set up as a visitor center. However the staff there are always happy to answer questions and direct you to the best spots. Oh yes, and a really big surprise is waiting for you at one end of the tract—a Caddo Indian Temple has been found there! To us it is nothing more than a large mound of dirt covered with trees, but to the experts it contains a wealth of valuable information and artifacts about the early Native American culture of Arkansas (ALL artifacts are protected!)

Did I mention that in the spring and summer there are miles of wide, sweeping prairie lands covered with wildflowers? If you are a photographer, be sure to bring along a lot of memory cards!

To reach the main entrance from I-30, take the Hwy. 278 exit (#30) at Hope and head north and then TURN LEFT onto Hwy. 73 towards Columbus. After 13 miles

Black-eyed Susans carpet the Grandview Prairie

you will enter the community of Columbus, then TURN RIGHT onto CR#35N. Go 1.9 miles and TURN RIGHT at the Conservation Center sign and up to the office (425039E, 3740450N). This is the main road into the property, and you are free to drive around as you like. If you continue straight on through, you will exit the property on the back side and come out to Hwy. 14, then turn right to loop back to Hwy. 73.

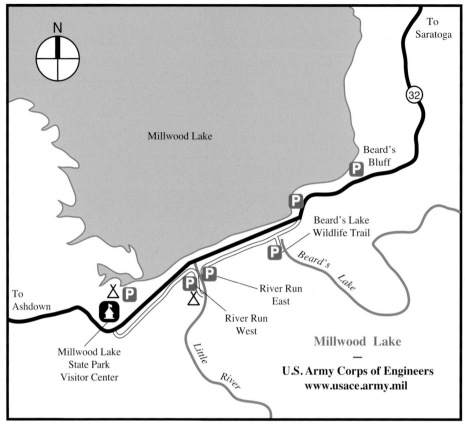

MILLWOOD LAKE is a giant lake in the southwest corner of Arkansas. One of the best bird photographers that I know, Charles Mills, spends a lot of time at this lake, and he produces some incredible wild bird photos. Now let's see — great photographer, great bird photos, spends a lot of time at Millwood — I would say go to Millwood Lake for birds! And how. You will always find tons of birds at this lake (as many as 333 species have been sighted), and they vary with the seasons. I like to spend time along the front edge of the dam and below the spillway (on both sides) and around the little state park nearby, always in the very early mornings and late evenings — that is when the birdlife is the most active. There is also a hiking trail at the state park (you just might see an alligator there!), and various other scenic attractions around this monster lake, including an interpretive Arboretum Trail and Watchable Wildlife Boardwalk at the Beard's Lake Area, which is located just below the eastern end of the dam. And you can watch the sunset right from the road along the top of the dam, or from the Beard's Bluff overlook. This lake has a very open, welcome, and inviting feel to it, and it is a great place to go spend some time at. You might run into Charles there making another great bird photo.

To get to Millwood Lake from Texarkana, take Hwy. 71 north to Ashdown, then TURN RIGHT onto Hwy. 32 and follow it about six miles to the state park and damsite area. From there the possibilities are endless!

Sunset from the dam (above); great egret (below)

River Valley Region

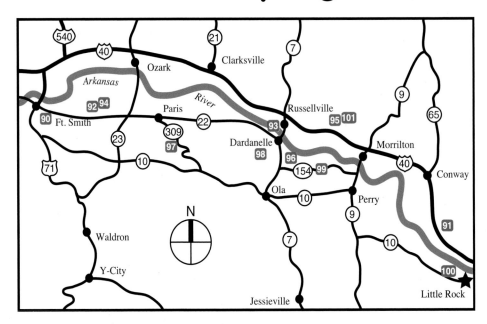

The RIVER VALLEY REGION of Arkansas has flat lands of prairies that are carpeted with wildflowers in the summertime, but it also has a string of high-mountain state parks that include the highest point in Arkansas. A brand new multi-million dollar visitor center at the edge of Ft. Smith provides educational facilities for scores of school kids and adults alike. There are wildlife areas where you can see bald eagles and huge flocks of geese and ducks and all sorts of wading birds and other feathered friends. And we have swamps too, my favorite new scenic destinations.

90 Scenic Areas in the River Valley Region

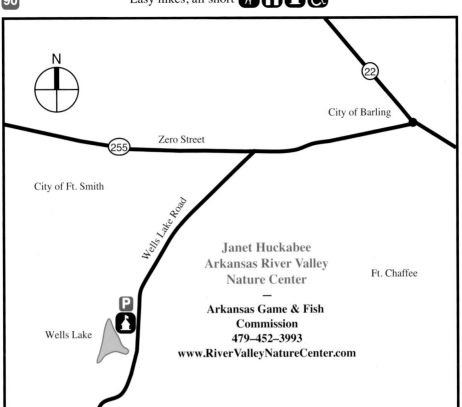

Janet Huckabee ARKANSAS RIVER VALLEY NATURE CENTER is the third nature center to be built by the Arkansas Game and Fish Commission and it seems they just keep getting better! This one is located on a 170-acre plot right next to Wells Lake, outside of Ft. Smith on what used to be part of the Ft. Chaffee Military Base. There are six hiking trails, including two that are wheelchair accessible, one going all the way around the lake, and plenty of areas for wildlife viewing. Ft. Chaffee is known for its large deer population, and so this will be a great area to come to look for deer. Inside there are some really great exhibits and both you and your kids will be able to spend hours learning about the Arkansas River Valley. There are tons of fun and interesting programs given by the center staff throughout the year (closed on Mondays). And if you are a school child in the area, oh my goodness, they have so many great school programs for classes—I almost wish I were back in school again!

To get to the center from I-40, take the Fort Smith/Van Buren exit #7 onto I-540. Go south 11 miles to exit #11, Zero Street (Hwy. 255), TURN LEFT onto Zero Street. Travel just over 4 miles, and TURN RIGHT on Veterans Avenue. TURN RIGHT at the first stop sign, on Ft. Smith Blvd. Follow Ft. Smith Blvd, which turns into Wells Lake Road, approximately 2 miles. The Nature Center and Wells Lake will be on the right. NOTE: the new I-49 will pass right by the center when constructed and these directions may change—just follow the signs once you get close!

White-tailed deer doe

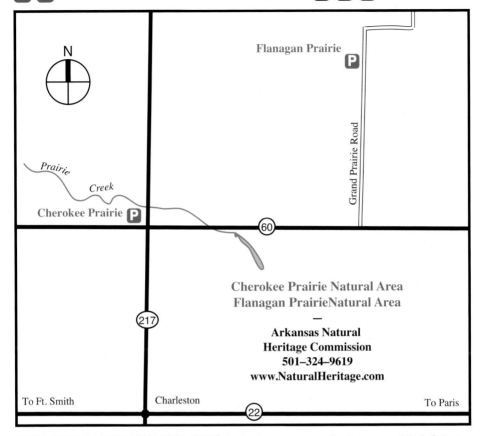

CHEROKEE PRAIRIE NATURAL AREA is the largest tract of tallgrass prairie left in Arkansas (566 acres). And when the flowers are blooming it can be one magical place for sure! The area is covered with an impressive array of tall grasses, including big bluestem, which can get several feet high, and tons of wildflowers, including a dense population of yellow coneflowers, as you can see in the photo at right. You will find lots of "prairie mounds" too, some up to three feet tall and over 40 feet wide. I used to think that these were actually places where Indians put their teepees on, but actually they are quite natural, but no one is certain how the mounds occurred. They are visible evidence that a tract has never been plowed or leveled. There is also a small stream running through the middle of this prairie—a rare thing these days.

Much of this area was once prairie land, but when settlers moved in, most of that was put under cultivation or altered in some way. A few small tracts were set aside for raising hay and have retained their original flora and soil structure and are now our only remaining prairies. Come early to this prairie, let the rising sun fill your heart with joy!

To reach Cherokee Prairie, take Hwy. 217 north out of Charleston for two miles to the intersection of Hwy. 60—there is a small parking area on the corner and the natural area is spread out in front of you. (UTM 405645E, 3910530N)

FLANAGAN PRAIRIE NATURAL AREA is another great example of what our tallgrass prairies used to look like. If you catch it at the right time, you'll find tons of wildflowers blooming there as far as you can see. The last time I visited, I found nearly two dozen different species in bloom. The best way to view these prairies is simply to get out and

larkspur (below left) & wild onion (below right) at Flanagan Prairie

wander around and you will discover all sorts of neat things. Sometimes you will run into a pocket of a particular species of wildflowers in bloom just in a certain area, or a spot that contains a dozen different types of blooms all together. Wander around and remember what our wide-open prairies used to look like.

To reach Flanagan Prairie, take Hwy. 217 north out of Charleston for two miles and TURN RIGHT onto Hwy. 60 (at the Cherokee Prairie parking lot). Go east for 2.2 miles and TURN LEFT onto Grand Prairie Road, then travel 1.5 miles north and the parking area and prairie are on the left. (UTM 409384E, 3913117N)

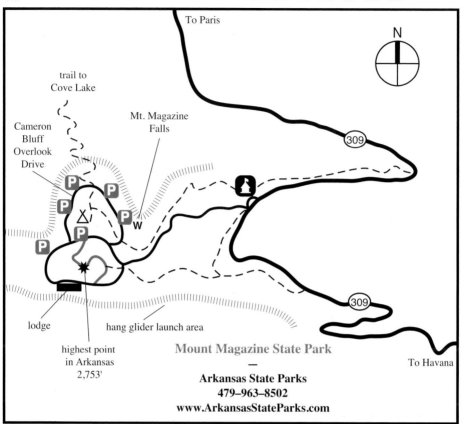

To Paris

N

trail to
Cove Lake

Mt. Magazine
Falls

Cameron
Bluff
Overlook
Drive

309

W

309

lodge

hang glider launch area

highest point
in Arkansas
2,753'

Mount Magazine State Park
—
Arkansas State Parks
479–963–8502
www.ArkansasStateParks.com

To Havana

MOUNT MAGAZINE STATE PARK is our newest state park, but it arrived with a bang! Not only is it the highest point in the state (2,753 feet), not only is it the main stomping grounds for the rare and beautiful Diana butterfly, but it is now home to one of the most impressive lodges in this part of the country! Book a room or cabin on the edge of the bluff and enjoy a long stay at this park, and you will find so much to see and do. Hike the trail up to the high point in the state (UTM 441308E, 3891558N), or the other many and varied trails that criss-cross this mountaintop park. Spend some time chasing butterflies and see if you can find the elusive Diana. There are also seasonal waterfalls, incredible views from the giant bluff that rims the mountain, bears roaming around, and a visitor center that is filled with exhibits and has interpretive programs throughout the year. And there are special hang glider launching sites, so you may spot a really giant bird out there soaring around. Oh yes, and Mt. Magazine is also home to the International Butterfly Festival each summer—it is the king of butterfly parks in Arkansas for sure (or with Diana in residence, should I say Queen?).

The park is located south of the Arkansas River, between Ft. Smith and Russellville on scenic Hwy. 309—17 miles south of Paris or 10 miles north of Havana.

*Weathered cedar
along the top of the
bluff below the lodge
(above); male Diana
fritillary butterfly (left)*

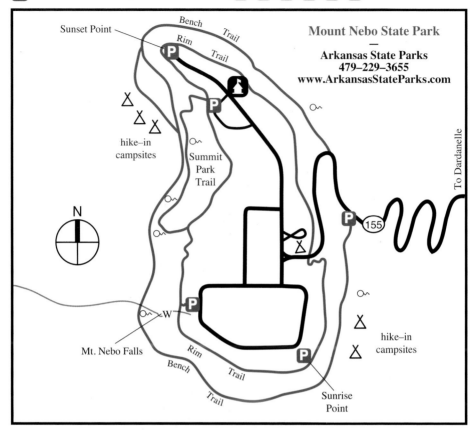

Mount Nebo State Park
—
Arkansas State Parks
479–229–3655
www.ArkansasStateParks.com

Sunset Point
Bench Trail
Rim Trail
hike–in campsites
Summit Park Trail
N
Mt. Nebo Falls
Rim Bench Trail
Trail
To Dardanelle
155
hike–in campsites
Sunrise Point

MOUNT NEBO STATE PARK is the second in a line of three mountaintop parks located along the Arkansas River. One of my favorite things about this park is the fact you have great views of both sunrise and sunsets (at locations called Sunrise Point and Sunset Point!). There are many hiking trails, including two that go around the entire mountain—one part way down the mountain called the Bench Trail (open to mountain bikes), and my favorite one that runs along the top of the bluffline for some of the best views in the state. There is also a seasonal waterfall (Mt. Nebo Falls, UTM 476442E, 3896892N), and lots of recreational activities for everyone. Hiking is the main activity here, and besides the views you can see all sorts of wildlife on the ground and up in the air if you are quiet and keep your eyes open. The park is used as a launch site for hang gliders, so you might see some non-natural birds hanging around. Oh yes, and there are many rental cabins available that line the bluff where you have some stunning views—you may never want to leave your cabin.

The park is located seven miles west of Dardanelle—take Hwy. 22 then TURN LEFT onto Hwy. 155. NOTE: the road near the top is the worst/most incredible curving paved road I have ever seen, and not recommended for long RV's—it does make for a terrific bike ride down the mountain though!

Sunrise from the Rim Trail (above); cascade above Mt. Nebo Falls (below)

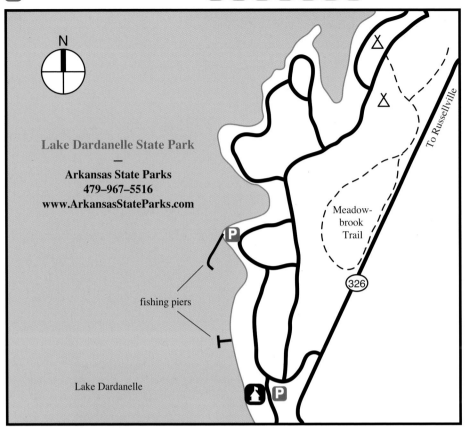

LAKE DARDANELLE STATE PARK is located at the edge of Russellville, along the shoreline of the vast 34,000-acre Lake Dardanelle. There is a hiking trail, campground, and bass fishing tournament facilities here, but what really interests me is the large visitor center that sits right on the edge of the lake, and the surrounding grounds. There are many exhibits inside the center, including four aquatic exhibits where young and old alike can learn, plus you have a great view of the lake. I like to wander around outside just before sunset—something about this place keeps drawing me back for more. There are tons of ducks and geese and wading birds hanging out, and there are bald eagles and ospreys patrolling the skies. Just recently a pair of bald eagles has built a nest—it is located across the lake and is easily visible from a boat. Bring your fishing pole or boat, or rent a kayak or bike, and watch the day disappear into the surrounding mountains.

To reach the park, take exit #81 on I-40 at Russellville and go south on Hwy. 7 for just one block, then TURN RIGHT onto Hwy. 326 and go five miles to the park entrance.

Lake Dardanelle sunset; osprey and bass (inset)

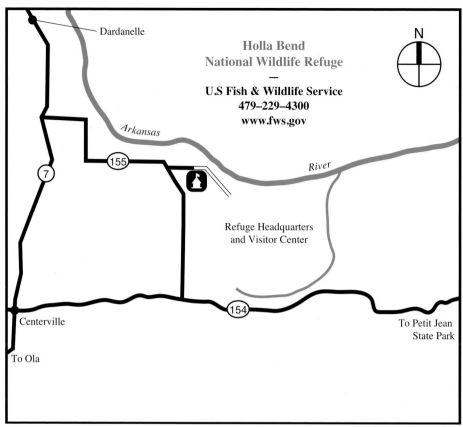

HOLLA BEND NATIONAL WILDLIFE REFUGE is the king for viewing flocks of water-fowl in the winter, in fact there are often flocks of tens of thousands of snow geese and ducks there at a time! The birds spend the night at the refuge, then fly out to other feeding grounds during the day, filling the air with wings. Bald eagles like to eat geese and ducks, so there are always eagles in the refuge during the winter months. There are also many other species of birds (236) and other wildlife, and some of the fields along the roads are great places to watch hawks at work. There are plenty of deer, raccoons and other mammals roaming around as well. In short, this is a photographer's paradise if you are interested in wildlife photos. There is a small visitor center, with friendly staff that are always eager to help you find the wildlife.

To reach Holla Bend, take Hwy. 7 south from the McDonalds in Dardanelle and go 2.6 miles and then TURN LEFT on Hwy. 155. Go 4.1 miles and you will come to the entrance road and gate on the LEFT. There is an entrance fee, but it is good for an entire year. The gates open at different times during the year, but always in plenty of time to be on hand for early photos and wildlife watching. The best times to visit are December through early spring.

Snow geese take flight

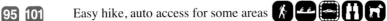
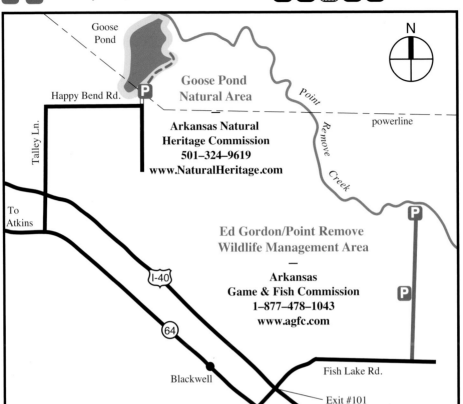

GOOSE POND NATURAL AREA contains a cypress-tupelo swamp that is the closest swamp that I know of to the Ozark mountains. It is located just east of Atkins right off of I-40 within the Point Remove Wildlife Management Area. When you first drive up to the little parking area you won't think much (UTM 513294E, 3901942N), but you can get out and walk around and see a really neat swamp area, thick with cypress and tupelo trees, and some cypress knees too. The actual "pond" area is right in front of the parking area (on your left as you arrive, with power lines going overhead), and what I like to do is hike around the right side where there is an elevated forest that is normally always dry (no trail—you'll be bushwhacking). There are good views into the swamp all along there, and you'll also pass under some giant oak trees that will tower above you. If you wander around a lot, you may find some of the water lily marshes too. In the wintertime, you are likely to see flocks of ducks and geese.

To get to the Goose Pond area, take the Atkins exit #94 and go east on Hwy. 64 for 3.8 miles and TURN LEFT onto Talley Lane. (Or take the Blackwell exit #101, go towards Hwy. 64 and turn right on Hwy. 64 for 2.8 miles and turn right onto Talley Lane). Then go 1.3 miles (passing under the interstate) and TURN RIGHT onto Happy Bend Road. Go one mile and TURN LEFT at the sharp curve and follow the little gravel road to the parking area.

ED GORDON/POINT REMOVE WILDLIFE MANAGEMENT AREA also contains vast open fields and water areas where you can see many flocks of wintering birds, plus tons of wading birds along Point Remove Creek and in the nearby marshes all year long.

Evening light at Goose Pond (above)
Great egret with a snack (below)

To get to the best bird-viewing areas of the management area, take the Blackwell exit #101 on I-40 and go north on Fish Lake Road for about a mile, then TURN LEFT at the sign. This road goes for about a mile and a half with open fields and marshes on both sides, and ends at Point Remove Creek—some great wading bird areas at the end of the road! (UTM 517835E, 3900021N)

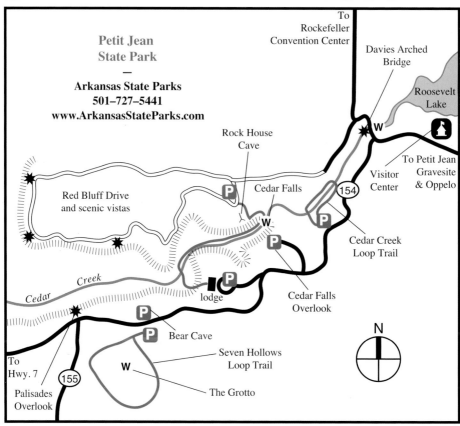

PETIT JEAN STATE PARK is the oldest and grandest of all our state parks, and you could easily spend a week or a month exploring all that it has to offer. Gosh, I really don't know where to begin, but I will highlight some of my favorite haunts I head for when I visit, which is pretty often. Sunrise at Petit Jean's Grave—one of the best in the entire state, with a view looking over a large bend in the Arkansas River. There are hiking trails galore—Seven Hollows Trail visits countless rock formations and "The Grotto" waterfall. Right across the road from that trailhead is the shortest trail called Bear Cave that kids will love—some really interesting rock formations. I really like to hike the Cedar Creek Loop Trail which takes you across the always interesting Cedar Creek twice, where you will find a boulder-strewn paradise. And, of course, the granddaddy of them all is the Cedar Creek Falls Trail, which visits the base of one of the greatest waterfalls in Arkansas, Cedar Falls (begin this hike at the rear of Mather Lodge). The climb back out of this one is pretty steep, but it is well worth the effort. I've been to Cedar Falls, oh, I don't know, probably more than a 100 times and I keep coming back!

Many of the buildings, bridges and trails were built in the 1930's by the Civilian Conservation Corps and this park is perhaps one of the best examples of their craftsmanship. Two spots to look for are the old stone water tower that is right at the entrance to the lodge—go open the door and peek inside; and the Davies Bridge over Cedar Creek near the visitor center—go have a look from streamside level at the beautiful stone arch, and the waterfall on the other side! You will also see their stone work all over the park. There is fine dining and beautiful views at Mather Lodge, and also many rental cabins that have great views down into the Cedar Creek canyon.

Cedar Falls (above); sunrise from Petit Jean Gravesite (below)

For westbound travelers on I-40, take exit #108 at Morrilton and go nine miles south on Hwy. 9, then TURN RIGHT at Oppelo and go 12 miles west on Hwy. 154 to the park. For eastbound travelers on I-40 take exit #81 at Russellville and go south on Hwy. 7 for 10 miles to Centerville and TURN LEFT onto Hwy. 154 for 16 miles.

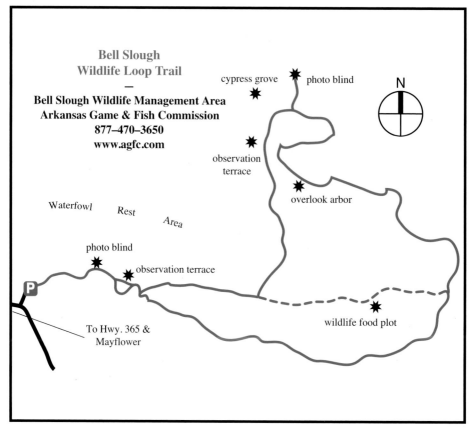

Bell Slough
Wildlife Loop Trail
—
Bell Slough Wildlife Management Area
Arkansas Game & Fish Commission
877–470–3650
www.agfc.com

cypress grove   photo blind

N

observation
terrace

overlook arbor

Waterfowl   Rest   Area

photo blind

observation terrace

P

To Hwy. 365 &
Mayflower

wildlife food plot

BELL SLOUGH WILDLIFE LOOP TRAIL visits a waterfowl rest stop area, which means you'll find thousands of ducks and geese and all sorts of critters here in the wintertime. There is a 2.3-mile easy loop trail that visits several wildlife observation areas that have been set up as blinds for wildlife watching and photography. It is a pretty nice hike even when there are no ducks around, especially since it is right off of the interstate and makes a great place to get out and stretch your legs awhile during a long car trip. This was one of the first areas to be developed by the Arkansas Game and Fish Commission as a "watchable wildlife" area, to demonstrate their commitment to non-game species, and to enhance our enjoyment of them.

To get to Bell Slough, take exit #135 on I-40 at Mayflower, then head south on Hwy. 365 through Mayflower. Continue south out of town and TURN LEFT onto Grassy Lake Road at the sign, which will take you under the interstate, and finally TURN LEFT and park at the trailhead (UTM 553158E, 3866263N). NOTE: during periods of high water the trail system may be flooded.

Canada goose and goslings

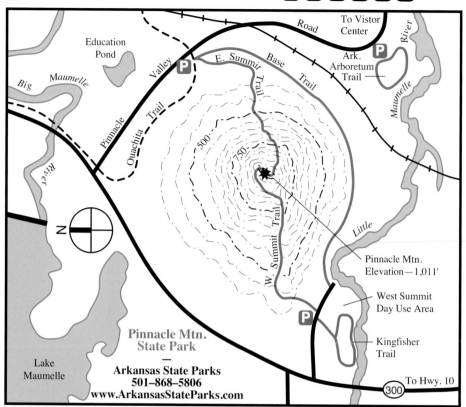

PINNACLE MOUNTAIN STATE PARK is another great park with tons of places to visit and things to do. It is the only park that I know of that has both a towering mountain to climb AND cypress swamps! There are hiking trails everywhere, the most popular being the Summit Trail that climbs steeply to the top of Pinnacle Mountain (a great exercise trail), and the easy, wheelchair-accessible Kingfisher Trail that visits some giant cypress trees along the Little Maumelle River. The Arkansas Arboretum Trail takes you through several different habitat zones where you will see a wide variety of trees and especially lots of wildflowers. There is a boat ramp and you can paddle your canoe for a couple miles downstream through a beautiful cypress swamp. There are more hiking trails at the visitor center (located on a different mountain nearby), and the center has some great exhibits and programs all during the year, including eagle watch programs. Oh, and be sure to look out for alligators if you go near the water!

     To get to the park, take the Hwy. 10 exit from I-430 (exit #9) and go west for seven miles, then TURN RIGHT on Hwy. 300 at the sign and go two miles—the main dayuse area will be on the right, but you will need to drive around a little bit to find the rest of the park. NOTE: this is a dayuse only park and the gates are locked soon after sunset, but there is camping at the nearby Corps of Engineers park, right on the Arkansas River. And for one of the few places in Arkansas where you can photograph a reflection of a mountain in a calm lake, visit the Education Pond, located across the road from the East Summit Trailhead (UTM 547616E, 3856029N).

Sunset from Little Maumelle River looking towards Pinnacle Mtn. (above, about a mile downstream from the West Summit boat ramp); sunrise on Pinnacle Mtn. from the Education Pond (below)

Little Rock Nature Centers

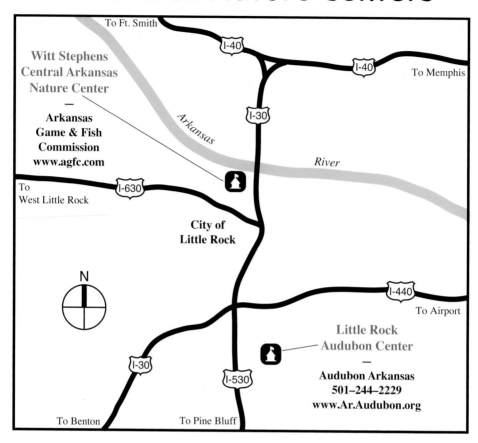

LITTLE ROCK NATURE CENTERS. We now have two large, expensive, and wonderful new nature centers at opposite ends of our capitol city. One is the fourth center constructed and managed by the Arkansas Game and Fish Commission—the Witt Stephens Central Arkansas Nature Center (602 President Clinton Avenue). It is located on the banks of the Arkansas River, in River Park, and has an impressive display of exhibits inside, as well as many things to see and do outside.

The second nature center is maintained by Audubon Arkansas, and is located at the southeast edge of Little Rock near Gillam Park (4500 Springer Blvd.). This facility includes wonderful educational features both inside and out and is a destination for young and old alike throughout the year.

For the latest information about both of these nature centers check out their respective web pages listed on the map above.

About the Author

It was more than 30 years ago when I first thought about producing a guidebook like this. I was just a kid then trying to feel my way around in the world, and realizing in a hurry that Arkansas is where I wanted to live and work and play. I took it on as my personal responsibility to explore and discover and photograph as many great scenic locations in this state as I could, and then share those images (and directions) with you. I want everyone to know the wilderness as I do, to gain a sense of appreciation for the wonderful natural world that we have around us, in hopes that one day you will do something that might help save a tree or flower or waterfall from destruction. That's my job.

A few years ago I moved into a log cabin at the edge of the Buffalo River wilderness in northwest Arkansas to be closer to my work. That is where I remain, with my beautiful bride, Pamela, and our daughter, Amber (along with an assortment of pets and wildlife). A barred owl has been hooting up a storm right outside my cabin window tonight as I try to complete work on this book—he is one of many natural wonders I have yet to photograph. Since I just rolled over 56 years I guess I've still got a few years left to wander around in the wilderness, seeking out even more new places to visit, and returning to special ones over and over again (chasing an owl or two along the way). This book is filled with those places, and if you visit them often you'll probably run into me one day. To keep up with my travels, you can read the Cloudland Journal, an online diary of life here that I've been writing since 1998. You can also order all of our publications, get info on photo workshops, and lots more at www.TimErnst.com.

I hope you get to explore many of the amazing scenic areas in this guidebook and have a great time doing it. Share your time with a child along the way as you do, and help lay the foundation for the next generation to insure these areas remain protected. Happy Trails to you!

The author hard at work, drifting in the lilies and cypress at Cane Creek State Park

Maps Legend

——————— Main Trail or Scenic Highway	**P** Main Parking Area
– – – – – Main Route—Bushwhack	**P** Other Parking
- - - - - Other Trails or Routes	**A** Visitor Center
--------- Alternate Bushwhack Route	**W** Waterfall
≈≈≈ Creek, Streams, Rivers	∩ Y Spring, Cave
Lake, Swamp/Bayou	✳ Point of Interest
	/|||||||| Bluffline
▬▬▬ Paved Road	X ✝ Campground, Cemetery
═══ Gravel Road	(I-40) Interstate Highway
= = = = Jeep Road	(23) (341) State/County Road-Paved/Gravel
● ■ Town, Building	[1003] Gravel Forest Road

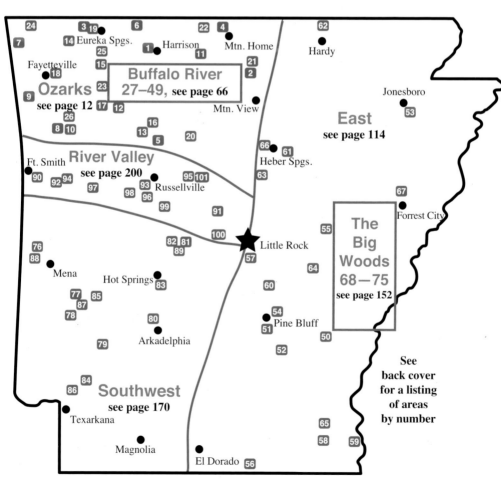

224